The Modern Memory of the Military-religious Orders

This volume examines the pervasive and persistent appropriations of the military orders across a broad chronology and several regions, including Mexico, Brazil, and Greece, areas beyond the traditional focus of prior research in medievalism.

Templars, Hospitallers, and Teutonic Knights, the military orders are among the most iconic aspects of the crusades and several still survive as chivalric honours or charitable organisations. In popular culture, the orders, particularly the Templars, have been the subject of or inspiration for films, books, television, and video games, from *Star Wars* to *The Da Vinci Code* and *Assassin's Creed*. In this volume, an overview of the early legacies of the military orders in the seventeenth and eighteenth centuries is followed by studies of the Templar conspiracy theories of Rosslyn Chapel, the Venerable Order of St John's creation of a medieval past, the legacy of the Hospitallers in modern Greece, the military orders in nineteenth-century Mexico, and the use of the Knights Templar by the far-right in Bolsonaro's Brazil. Ultimately, it expands the scope of the field and indicates further avenues for research.

The Modern Memory of the Military-religious Orders is a valuable resource for students and scholars of the crusades, the military orders, and medievalism.

Rory MacLellan is a postdoctoral research fellow at Historic Royal Palaces. He specialises in medieval religious history, especially the crusades and the military-religious orders. His first book is *Donations to the Knights Hospitaller in Britain and Ireland, 1291–1400* (2021).

ENGAGING THE CRUSADES

THE MEMORY AND LEGACY OF THE CRUSADES

SERIES EDITORS

JONATHAN PHILLIPS & MIKE HORSWELL

Engaging the Crusades

The Memory and Legacy of the Crusades

Series Editors: Jonathan Phillips and Mike Horswell, Royal Holloway, University of London, UK.

Engaging the Crusades is a series of volumes which offer initial windows into the ways in which the crusades have been used in the last two centuries; demonstrating that the memory of the crusades is an important and emerging subject. Together these studies suggest that the memory of the crusades, in the modern period, is a productive, exciting and much needed area of investigation.

In this series:

The Making of Crusading Heroes and Villains
Engaging the Crusades, Volume Four
Edited by Mike Horswell and Kristin Skottki

Playing the Crusades
Engaging the Crusades, Volume Five
Edited by Robert Houghton

Tales of the Crusaders – Remembering the Crusades in Britain
Engaging the Crusades, Volume Six
Elizabeth Siberry

The Modern Memory of the Military-religious Orders
Engaging the Crusades, Volume Seven
Edited by Rory MacLellan

For more information about this series, please visit:
https://www.routledge.com/Engaging-the-Crusades/book-series/ETC

The Modern Memory of the Military-religious Orders

Engaging the Crusades, Volume Seven

Edited by
Rory MacLellan

Routledge
Taylor & Francis Group

LONDON AND NEW YORK

First published 2022
by Routledge
4 Park Square, Milton Park, Abingdon, Oxon OX14 4RN

and by Routledge
605 Third Avenue, New York, NY 10158

Routledge is an imprint of the Taylor & Francis Group, an informa business

British Library Cataloguing-in-Publication Data
A catalogue record for this book is available from the British Library

Library of Congress Cataloging-in-Publication Data
A catalog record has been requested for this book

ISBN: 978-1-032-06119-1 (hbk)
ISBN: 978-1-032-06120-7 (pbk)
ISBN: 978-1-003-20080-2 (ebk)

DOI: 10.4324/9781003200802

Typeset in Times New Roman
by codeMantra

Contents

Figures

Contributors

Ignacio García Lascurain Bernstorff was born in Mexico City in 1988. He studied in Freiburg im Breisgau, Munich and Rome and earned in 2019 his PhD in History from the University of Munich. He currently works at the Vatican City-based Römisches Institut der Görres-Gesellschaft and teaches at the University of Potsdam.

Luiz Felipe Anchieta Guerra is an independent scholar. He specialises in medievalism, particularly the misuse of the medieval past by the Brazilian far-right, and has published on this topic in both English and Portuguese.

Nigel Hankin is an independent scholar. He studied for an MSt in Literature and Art at Kellogg College, Oxford, his dissertation for which forms the basis of his chapter in this volume. He is now reading for an MA in Classics at King's College London.

Rory MacLellan is a postdoctoral research fellow at Historic Royal Palaces. He specialises in medieval religious history, especially the crusades and the military-religious orders. His first book, *Donations to the Knights Hospitaller in Britain and Ireland, 1291–1400*, is published by Routledge.

Photeine V. Perra is an assistant professor in Medieval History at the University of the Peloponnese. She studied History at Ionian University (Corfu) and completed her PhD thesis at Aegean University (Department of Mediterranean Studies-Rhodes). Her research interests are focused on the study of the Latin Rule in Greek lands (1204–1797), the Hospitallers' presence in Greece, and the relations between Byzantium and Venice and between Venice and the Ottoman Empire. She is a contributor to the *Encyclopaedic Prosopographical Lexicon of Byzantine History and Civilization* and a member of the editorial committee of the journal *Domus Byzantinus*, while she has published several articles and book presentations in various journals in Greece and abroad, as well as chapters in the multivolume *History of the Greek people.*

Lizzie Swarbrick is a Leverhulme Early Career Fellow in the School of Art History, University of Edinburgh. Her work re-examines Rosslyn Chapel as an important 15th-century church and as a mutable cultural monument. More generally, she works on art and architecture from Scotland c.1250-1560. Lizzie was educated at the University of St Andrews and the Courtauld Institute of Art.

Acknowledgements

This book was born out of the disruption of the COVID pandemic. Faced with a seemingly never-ending period of COVID-induced furlough (eventually lasting 13 months) from my postdoctoral project, the organisation of this book became my main furlough project. I am immensely grateful to all the contributors for their chapters, created under difficult circumstances and with often limited archival access due to the pandemic. Together, they have created a range of fascinating chapters that push the boundaries of the field, expanding the study of crusade medievalism to new geographic regions and offering new perspectives on old ones. Thanks also to Laura Pilsworth and Izzy Voice for their forbearance in the delays to this volume, and to Mike Horswell for his advice and support throughout the process.

Introduction

Rory MacLellan

Though only arising in the aftermath of the First Crusade (1095–99), the military-religious orders soon came to dominate the crusading movement. While not technically crusaders themselves, not having sworn a crusade vow, these groups of soldier-monks would become mainstays of each major crusade expedition to the Eastern Mediterranean. They also saw service in the other main crusade theatres: Iberia, North Africa, and the Baltic. In the guise of the Knights Hospitaller, they could even be argued to have carried on the crusade well into the early modern period, until the order was expelled from Malta by Napoleon in 1798.

The military orders retain an enduring appeal. They are the subject of two regular conferences, one in the UK, the other in Poland, and feature regularly in crusade scholarship and other connected fields. Several military orders are still with us today as religious orders, chivalric orders, or charitable foundations, or a combination thereof, such as the Teutonic Order and several successors to the medieval Hospitallers, including the Sovereign Military Order of Malta, the Venerable Order of St John, and the three Johanniterorden.

Fiction is rife with orders of knight-monks, whether the Jedi Knights of *Star Wars*, or actual Templars in *Assassin's Creed* and *The Da Vinci Code*. But this fame has also led to darker appropriations. The imagery of the Teutonic Knights was adopted by Nazi Germany, particularly in its occupation of Poland and the Baltic, the order's former stomping ground. As chapters in this volume show, other military orders have also been appropriated, with Fascist Italy making use of the Hospitallers during their occupation of Rhodes, whilst the far-right in both contemporary UK and Brazil is enamoured with the Templars.

But despite the persistent presence of the military orders in fiction, popular history, and academic study, and their political misuse in both the previous centuries and today, their post-medieval legacies

DOI: 10.4324/9781003200802-1

have been largely overlooked. This collection is the first dedicated specifically to the modern memory of the military orders, pointing a way forward for scholars of crusade medievalism to bring this important aspect of the crusades further into the field.

The early memorialisation of the orders in Britain, which, along with the US, has been the country addressed most by scholars of crusade medievalism thus far, is dealt with in the first chapter of this volume. It focuses on how the military orders were remembered in four popular historical works of the seventeenth and eighteenth centuries, when they first became the subject of antiquarian study. This serves to bridge the gap between the orders' medieval origins and the following chapters, which deal with the nineteenth through to the twenty-first centuries.

Lizzie Swarbrick uses an art-historical perspective to examine the long history of Templar conspiracy theories at Rosslyn Chapel, from the Freemasons to *The Da Vinci Code*, and how this has been exploited by the contemporary far-right. She offers a concise and comprehensive debunking of conspiratorial interpretations of the church's famous 'Templar' carvings.

Nigel Hankin's chapter concludes this initial focus on the legacy of the orders in Britain, discussing the Victorian Venerable Order of St John's construction of a medieval identity by their collecting of medieval Hospitaller artefacts and occupation of Hospitaller sites. They then used this medieval past to build a historical justification for medical activities like the St John Ambulance, the export of which to colonies abroad saw the Venerable Order become part of the network of empire.

The following three chapters expand the volume's focus to countries that have seen little attention in English language scholarship on crusade medievalism. Photeine Perra offers the first academic study of the legacy of the orders in modern Greece. This ground-breaking piece focuses on the reception of the Hospitallers in the country, particularly in Rhodes and the Dodecanese. Perra demonstrates how that order's history there presents a fascinating conundrum. It can neither be fully cast as one of alien invaders, as it can in the Muslim world, nor can the Hospitallers be easily adopted as part of Greece's own historical identity, as Catholic countries such as Malta have done, because of their confessional and cultural differences. In addition, the Italian occupation of the island (1912–43) and their restoration of many Hospitaller monuments later left the order tainted by association with Fascist Italy. Instead of being adopted as enemies or ancestors, the Hospitallers are largely disregarded by most Rhodiots.

Ignacio García Lascurain Bernstorff takes our focus to the Americas, examining the place of the military orders in nineteenth-century Mexico, where the newly independent country sought three times to create a military order of its own. Meanwhile, several Mexicans continued to emphasise their connections to Spain through their membership of the Spanish military orders.

Finally, Luiz Felipe Anchieta Guerra's chapter brings the legacy of the military orders right up to the present day, examining how they have been adopted by the Brazilian far-right and in particular supporters of Brazil's President Jair Bolsonaro. Through a study of memes and eccentric publicity stunts, he shows how the actual veracity of these medievalisms, or the fact that Brazil lacks a medieval history of its own, does not mean that they should be dismissed out of hand but subjected to serious study.

Together, the chapters point towards several potential avenues for future research: the early formation of the memory of the military orders in the early modern period beyond Britain; the debunking of classic Templar pseudohistories; the collecting habits of the Order of Malta and other surviving military orders; the modern perception of military orders in their former territories; the creation of military orders to solidify new national identities; political crusade medievalism in countries without a medieval or crusade history. These are all valuable lines of inquiry and will help elucidate further not only the military orders and their place in history, but also the wider consequences and importance of the crusade movement in which they played a key role.

1 Memories of the Military Orders in Britain in the Seventeenth and Eighteenth Centuries

Rory MacLellan

Most studies of the modern memories of the crusades focus on the nineteenth and twentieth centuries, particularly in Britain, a period in which the image of the military-religious orders was already well established as one of fierce soldiers, often mysterious and romantic, sometimes tragic or corrupt.[1] But when did these views of the medieval Templars, Hospitallers, and others first emerge? In omitting the early modern period, there is a risk of back-reading continuity into the middle memory of the orders. This chapter shall provide the first survey of how the military orders were remembered in Britain in the seventeenth and eighteenth centuries, when they first became the subject of historical study, focusing upon their depiction in four bestselling histories written in the period.

The Military Orders in Early Modern Britain

The military orders featured little in other seventeenth- and eighteenth-century British sources. They do not appear in cartoons of the period, even those referencing Napoleon's occupation of Malta, which he took from the Hospitallers in 1798.[2] Though the politician, general, and caricaturist George Townshend (1724–1807) sometimes signed himself 'A Knight of Malta', the order does not appear in his work.[3] Apart from a few seventeenth-century pamphlets, it is only from the 1720s that news of the order's activities begins to regularly appear in British newspapers.[4] Besides the 1633 edition of Marlowe's late sixteenth-century *The Jew of Malta*, the only other fiction touching upon the military orders and published in Britain before 1800 is the play *The Knight of Malta*, the poem *The Lady of Brumpton, and Knight of Malta*, and the novels *The Knight of Malta: or, the Reward of Constancy* and *Heloise: or, the Siege of Rhodes*.[5] Each of these deals with the Hospitallers. There do not appear to be any fictional treatments of the other military orders in this period.

DOI: 10.4324/9781003200802-2

I shall begin these case studies with Thomas Fuller's *The Historie of the Holy Warre*, published in 1639. The first history of the crusades in English, Fuller's work includes several chapters on the Templars, Hospitallers, and Teutonic Knights. By 1651, the book had already reached four editions.[6] Next, I will discuss Elias Ashmole's 1672 *The Institution, Laws and Ceremonies of the Most Noble Order of the Garter* which, despite its title, also includes one of the first attempts in English to provide a history of all the military orders, from the largest foundations to the smallest.[7] The *English Short Title Catalogue* (ESTC) lists eight editions of this book between 1672 and 1726. Moving on to the eighteenth century, I look at David Hume's *The History of England*, published in six volumes from 1754 to 1761, which provides brief accounts of the Templars and Hospitallers. His *History* had gone through over 100 editions and reprintings by the end of the following century.[8] Finally, I examine the image of the military orders in Edward Gibbon's six-volume *The Decline and Fall of the Roman Empire*, published from 1776 to 1788. The ESTC records over 25 reprints or editions of some or all of these volumes from 1776 to 1797.

These four histories were readily accessible to a wide readership, as they were all written in English and had a less specialist focus than other available accounts of the military orders, such as the 1728 English translation of the Abbé de Vertot's history of the Hospitallers.[9] In a period when, unlike the nineteenth century, they had little or no presence in British literature and theatre, these histories are among the best sources of depictions of the military orders in early modern Britain.

Fuller's *Historie of the Holy Warre*

Thomas Fuller (1607/1608–61) was a Cambridge cleric who advocated for political and religious moderation in the conflicts between crown, church, and parliament in the seventeenth century.[10] His first book, *The Historie of the Holy Warre* (1639), focuses primarily on the crusades from 1095 to 1291, with a supplement detailing the later history of the military orders, the causes behind the failure of the Holy Land crusades and the kingdom of Jerusalem, and accounts of important crusaders and the involvement of each of Europe's nations in the crusade movement.[11] He devotes several chapters to the Templars, Hospitallers, and Teutonic Knights.[12] He provides a broad history of each, even describing the very brief revival of the Hospitallers in England under Mary I, yet his account is often coloured by his anti-monasticism.[13]

Fuller initially presents the Hospitallers as a noble ideal, noting their role in protecting pilgrims, their vows of poverty, chastity, and obedience, their supposed neutrality in disputes between Christian rulers, and the order's prohibitions on usury and duelling. But this does not last: 'it is given to most religious orders, to be clear in the spring and mirie in the stream. These Hospitallers afterwards getting wealth, unlaced themselves from the strictnesse of their first Institution, and grew loose into all licentiousnesse'. He goes on to accuse the brethren of breaking their vows of poverty through the order's vast wealth, of obedience by rebelling against their initial superior, the patriarch of Jerusalem, and of chastity by living 'betwixt bawds and banquets'.[14] He later recounts the Hospitallers' conflict with Fulcher, patriarch of Jerusalem, including attacking the church of the Holy Sepulchre and bribing the college of cardinals to rule against Fulcher when he complained to them about the order.[15]

His account of the Templars also begins by presenting them as being born out of high ideals but falling into corruption as their wealth and power increased:

> From Alms-men they turned Lords; and though very valiant at first (for they were sworn rather to die then to flie) afterwards lazinesse withered their arms, and swelled their bellies. They laughed at the rules of their first Institution, as at the swaddling-clothes of their infancie.[16]

Fuller depicts the order as attempting to trick St Louis into making peace with Egypt for their own ends, but also wisely counselling Robert of Artois against his attack on Mansoura in the Fifth Crusade which ended in a disaster for the crusaders.[17] Despite his criticisms of the Templars' supposed corruption, Fuller condemns Clement V and Philip IV's actions in bringing about the end of the order: 'the Templars, by the cruel deed of Pope Clement the fifth, and foul fact of Philip the Fair King of France, were finally exstirpated out of all Christendome'.[18] He goes on to present both arguments for and against the guilt of the Templars on the charges of heresy that they faced, concluding 'let us suspend our censure till the day of judgement; and then and no sooner shall we certainly be informed therein'.[19] Despite this, he does list 'the Treacherie of the Templars' as one of the eight factors that hindered the crusades.[20] He also complains about the Pope exempting a supposed 'six and twentie thousand manours in Europe, belonging to the Templars and Hospitallers, from paying any tithes to the Priest of the parish; so that many a minister in England smarteth at this day for the Holy warre'. This exemption from tithes was 'sacriledge' as it took away 'the dowrie of the Church without assuring her any joynture in lieu of it'.[21] Here we may see Fuller's personal concerns shining through, being a minister reliant on tithes himself.

Fuller is wholly positive in his account of the Teutonic Knights, 'who behaved themselves right valiantly clean through the Holy Warre' and 'cannot be touched either for treason or faction'.[22] He praises the order's history in the Baltic, where they responsible for founding many cities and their former lands of Prussia and Livonia 'are now become the rich fringe of Europe'. The order 'in Prussia did knight-service against the Tartarians, and were Christendomes best bank against the inundations of those barbarous people'.[23] This shift to operating in Europe rather than the Holy Land is something Fuller also approves of in the Hospitallers, in marked contrast to his condemnation of their history in the Levant:

> to the terrour of the Turks, comfort of the Christians, and their own immortall fame, they maintained this Island [Rhodes], and secured the seas for the passage of Pilgrimes to Jerusalem: till at last in the yeare 1523, after six moneths siege they surrendred the citie to their own honour, and shame of other Christians who sent them no succour.[24]

He is also positive about their defence of Malta against the Turks:

> here the Hospitallers seated themselves, and are the bulwark of Christendome to this day, giving dayly evident proof of their courage. But their master-piece was in the yeare 1565, when they couragiously defended the citie of Malta besieged by Soliman.[25]

In contrast, Fuller condemns the Templars for not continuing to fight as the Hospitallers and Teutonic Order did after 1291. While he disliked the wealth of both these orders

> they busied themselves in defending of Christendome, maintaining the Island of Rhodes against the Turks, as the Teutonick order defended Spruce-land against the Tartarian; the world therefore never grudged them great wages who did good work. These were accounted necessarie members of Christendome, the Templars esteemed but a superfluous wenne; they lay at rack and manger and did nothing.[26]

In his shift from criticism to praise for the Hospitallers once they began to fight the Turks from Rhodes, we can see Fuller reflecting a wider concern in England about the power of the Ottoman Empire, which was also the subject of his book's final chapter.[27] Fear of the Ottoman advance can be seen in how the Hospitallers' victory over them in the siege of Malta in 1565 was celebrated even in Protestant England.[28] In 1571, the defeat of the Turks by a Catholic force at Lepanto was greeted with a sermon of thanksgiving in St Paul's Cathedral.[29] Richard Knolle's *The Generall Historie of the Turkes* (1603), the first English history of the Turks, also ends with a chapter on the contemporary Ottoman Empire, discussing the military strength of the Turks and what can be done to defeat them, much in the manner of a medieval recovery treatise.[30] Fuller also had personal reasons to be sympathetic to the Hospitallers combating the Turks and their allies in the Mediterranean. Serving then as a vicar in Dorset, Fuller would have been well aware of contemporary raids upon the West Country by the Barbary Corsairs.[31]

Readers of Fuller's history would come away with a mixed view of the military orders: 'some pietie, more loosenesse and lazinesse', as he described the membership of religious orders.[32] But he also thought that these supposedly corrupt and lazy institutions could be redeemed if they continued to fight to defend 'Christendom' after 1291, as the Hospitallers and Teutonic Knights did. Otherwise, they would become increasingly idle and be suppressed like the Templars.

Ashmole's *Order of the Garter*

Though Fuller does address the three major orders, he does not discuss the many more minor ones such as the order of St Lazarus, or regional orders like the Knights of Santiago. These and many others are included in Elias Ashmole's *The Institution, Laws and Ceremonies of the Most Noble Order of the Garter* (1672). An antiquarian, astrologer, alchemist, and founder of the Ashmolean Museum, Ashmole also had a great interest in heraldry and was Windsor Herald from 1660 to 1675. He was particularly enthused by the Order of the Garter, which he first began studying late in the Interregnum (1649–60). An ardent royalist, his interest may have in part been motivated as an act of resistance against the Protectorate, as well as the order's royal nature.[33]

The first three chapters of Ashmole's book deal with knighthood, its history and characteristics, and with other knightly orders besides the Order of the Garter. Chapter 2 addresses the military-religious orders, defining them and the motives behind their foundation, and giving very brief histories of each military order.[34] Ashmole claims that both military-religious orders (which he calls religious or ecclesiastical orders) and chivalric orders (which he refers to as military orders) were founded for three main purposes. First, out of 'perfect and sincere love to Honor', the 'continual advancement of Military Affairs', and to reward, 'excite and promote Virtue'. Second:

> to repel the violence and cruelty [of non-Christians], to vindicate the oppressed, redeem the injured and enslaved, to give entertainment and relief to Pilgrims and Strangers, were part of the Duties to which the Knights Hospitallers, Templers, and those of Saint Iames in Gallicia, stood engaged by their first foundation.
>
> A third reason was to fight in defence of the Christian Faith, against Pagans and Infidels, to propagate the Christian Territories, and to promote the service of the Catholick Church; which was the chief cause why the Orders last mentioned were instituted, as also those other of the Holy Sepulchre, Calatrava, Alcantara, St. Saviour of Mount Royal, our Lady of Montesa, of Christ in Portugal, and the Sword-Bearers in Livonia.[35]

Following this are brief individual histories of 46 different military-religious orders. Each typically notes the origins of the order, their purpose, rule, dress, and their fate, if dissolved, or current whereabouts, if still active. Ashmole often elides different institutions or creates entirely new ones that never existed. For example, one of the orders he describes are the Brician Knights, a Swedish military order dedicated to St Birgitta of Sweden.[36] His account is largely reproduced from that of Joseph Micheli y Marquez's 1642 *Tesoro Militar de Cavalleria*, another volume on the military-religious and chivalric orders.[37] Ashmole cites as his source a 'Marcus. Ant. Vianus' mentioned in Micheli y Marquez's book. But both he and Micheli y Marquez's other source for the Brician Knights, a Brother Antonius Bosius, either never existed or have since been lost and are unattested elsewhere. Though St Birgitta did write on the subject of knighthood, there is no medieval evidence of a military order dedicated to her.[38] An 1864 study of the Swedish peerage did record three knights of St Birgitta from just one family, the Ulfsparres, but later historians found that the entire medieval history of this family was fabricated.[39] Of the 46 orders listed by Ashmole, 21 either never existed, were proposed but never founded, or were not military orders at all but rather secular chivalric or non-military-religious orders.[40] Despite these inaccuracies, his account is the first comprehensive survey in English of each of the military orders, and remained the only one until F.C. Woodhouse's volume on the orders in 1879.[41]

Throughout these histories, Ashmole presents an almost uniformly positive view of the military orders. Only the Templars and Hospitallers come in for criticism, again due to a supposed corruption caused by their wealth:

> But when Riches increast, and their Revenues were augmented, they [the Templars] grew proud, and withdrew themselves from the obedience of the Patriarch of Ierusalem, to join with the Pope.[42]

Of the Hospitallers, he writes that 'when their Revenues increased, it begat a neglect of their former religious and humble carriage; and forthwith they laboured with the Pope to be absolved from their obedience to the Patriarch'. The patriarch and several other bishops then went to Rome to 'manifest the injuries they sustained from the Knights'.[43] This focus on both orders breaking their obedience to the patriarch builds upon Fuller's account of the Hospitallers' break with the patriarch by adding an anti-Papal undertone. Both orders' arrogance and greed is set alongside their preference for papal authority over patriarchal.

Despite these critiques, Ashmole agrees with Fuller that there was no basis to the crimes the Templars were accused of, instead saying that many 'sober men' judge 'that their Wealth was their greatest crime'. Unlike this earlier author, who accuses the Templars and Hospitallers of hindering the crusades with their infighting, Ashmole commends both orders for their defence of the kingdom of Jerusalem:

> These Knights, with those other of the Holy Sepulchre, Hospitallers, and Teutonicks, were the principal Columns which supported the Kingdom of Ierusalem, for a long time; and therefore their valiant encounters with the Infidels, and forwardness to sacrifice their lives, for the honor of God, and defence of the Holy Land, ought to be had in everlasting remembrance.[44]

He goes on to applaud the Hospitallers who had 'constantly hazarded their lives in the defence of the Christian Faith' and defended Rhodes from the Turks 'with exceeding great charge, and signal valor'.[45] On Malta, the Hospitallers 'yet continue the Bulwark and Fortress of Europe'.[46]

Of Philip de Mézières' proposed but never founded Order of the Passion, Ashmole notes the 'nobleness and largeness of the design'.[47] Ashmole also praises the Mercedarians, which he mistakenly identifies as a military order, for their role ransoming captives.[48] This was 'charitable and pious work', which the order continued to carry out 'with all religious care and faithfulness' since their foundation.[49]

On the other more minor orders, Ashmole is very matter of fact and provides little opinion or analysis of them, often being more concerned with their heraldry and dress than their activities, understandably, considering that Ashmole was a herald. For example, the entry for the probably fictitious Knights of St Blaise reads:

> These were called also Knights de Sancta Maria, and founded under the Rule of St. Basil. They were Officers and Servants to the Kings of Armenia, and had assigned them for their Habit Skie-colour, with a Cross gold, worn before their breasts. Others say a Red Cross, and in the middle thereof the Picture of St. Blase their Patron.
>
> This Order was at the height, when the Armenian Kings, of the House of Luzignam, kept their Court in the City of Acon.[50]

Hume's *History of England*

David Hume (1711–76), philosopher and historian, began his *History of England* (published 1754–61) as *The History of Great Britain, Volume I*, which dealt with the reigns of James I and Charles I.[51] The second volume covered the period from Charles' death through to 1688. It was only with the next two volumes, on the Tudors, that the series became *The History of England*. The final two volumes dealt with the invasion of Julius Caesar through to the reign of Henry VII. Though focused on English history, the series does take in more international topics such as the crusades and the military orders. His account of the crusades has been derided as 'hack work' but his brief depiction of the Templars and Hospitallers demonstrate interesting developments upon those of Fuller and Ashmole.[52] Like Fuller, Hume presents the Templars as being a noble ideal ('uniting the two qualities most popular of that age, devotion and valour') but sliding into laziness as their wealth increased:

> Their great riches, joined to the course of time, had, by degrees, relaxed the severity of these virtues [...] they rather chose to enjoy in ease their opulent revenues in Europe [...] and passed their time wholly in the fashionable amusements of hunting, gallantry, and the pleasures of the table.[53]

Despite these supposed flaws, Hume claims that there was no basis to the accusations made against the Templars at their trial.[54] This account of the Templars follows the same lines as Fuller and Ashmole, but Hume differs from both of these earlier authors when it comes to the Hospitallers. Rather than claiming that the order was corrupted by its wealth and fell into the same laziness and corruption as the Templars, Hume instead says that the Hospitallers were not wealthy at all: 'poverty had as yet preserved them from like corruptions'. The brethren of the order 'still distinguished themselves by their enterprizes against the infidels'.[55]

Like these earlier writers, he praises the Hospitallers' role in fighting non-Christians, though he includes their tenure in the Holy Land in this, a period of the order's history which Fuller derided. When describing the suppression of the order in England, Wales, and Ireland by Henry VIII in 1540, Hume writes that the Hospitallers had 'by their valour, done great service to Christendom; and had very much retarded, at Jerusalem, Rhodes, and Malta, the rapid progress of the barbarians'.[56] Hume's wholly positive view of the Hospitallers, compared to Fuller's more measured one, may in part be because Hume, not being a priest himself, was less concerned than Fuller at the order's exemption from tithes.

Gibbon's *Decline and Fall*

Edward Gibbon (1737–94), who corresponded with Hume and viewed the philosopher as a mentor, touched upon the military orders in his own historical writings.[57] His *The History of the Decline and Fall of the Roman Empire* (1776–88) begins in AD 98 with the reign of Trajan but goes through to the sixteenth century and so takes in both the crusades and the military orders. In Gibbon's depiction of the orders, we find a return to the view of Fuller and Ashmole that the Templars and Hospitallers were a noble ideal:

> But the firmest bulwark of Jerusalem was founded on the knights of the Hospital of St. John, and of the temple of Solomon; on the strange association of a monastic and military life, which fanaticism might suggest, but which policy must approve. The flower of the nobility of Europe aspired to wear the cross, and to profess the vows, of these respectable orders; their spirit and discipline were immortal.[58]

His approval of this combination of monastic and military stands in stark contrast to the disdain he displayed elsewhere for monasticism. In late imperial Rome 'the last remains of military spirit were buried in the cloister [...] and the soldiers' pay was lavished on the useless multitudes of both sexes who could only plead the merits of abstinence and chastity'.[59] Yet here, the active vocation of the military orders combined with 'useless' monasticism created an institution of 'spirit and discipline'.

Like our previous authors, Gibbon goes on to write that the Templars were corrupted by their wealth, as were (and here he disagrees with Hume) the Hospitallers:

> The austerity of the convent soon evaporated in the exercise of arms; the world was scandalized by the pride, avarice, and corruption of these Christian soldiers; their claims of immunity and jurisdiction disturbed the harmony of the church and state; and the public peace was endangered by their jealous emulation.[60]

Despite the supposed flaws of these orders, Gibbon writes that even 'in their most dissolute period' the Templars and Hospitallers 'maintained their fearless and fanatic character' and the 'spirit of chivalry' lived on in Hospitaller Malta.[61] Like Fuller, Ashmole, and Hume, Gibbon is full of praise for the Hospitallers' defence of Rhodes:

> under the discipline of the order, that island emerged into fame and opulence; the noble and warlike monks were renowned by land and sea: and the bulwark of Christendom provoked, and repelled, the arms of the Turks and Saracens.[62]

Of their tenure on Malta, he writes:

> Crete, or Candia, with Cyprus, and most of the smaller islands of Greece and Asia, have been subdued by the Turkish arms, whilst the little rock of Malta defies their power, and has emerged, under the government of its military Order, into fame and opulence.[63]

Again, the military orders, though previously lazy, arrogant, or corrupt, could redeem themselves by continuing to fight the Turks.

Conclusion

We can see a great deal of continuity here in the middle memory of the military orders. These knights were still portrayed as romantic but often corrupt warriors, much as nineteenth-century literature did, though perhaps with a greater emphasis on combating the Turks, spurred on by contemporary concerns about the Ottoman Empire.[64] For each of these four authors, even the strongly anti-Catholic Gibbon, the military orders arose out of noble ideals, yet ones that they struggled to live up to. For all four authors, the Templars were a cautionary example of what wealth and pride could do to an institution. While the Hospitallers sometimes fell into the same flaws, they were always redeemed by their defence of Rhodes and Malta. When the Teutonic Knights were mentioned, they were presented wholly positively, particularly their campaigns in the Baltic. In this praise of military orders 'defending Christendom', we can see the authors emulating contemporary concerns about the power of the Ottoman Empire, while their criticism of the orders, and of the Templars and Hospitallers' break from patriarchal authority in favour of the Pope, demonstrates their anti-Catholicism.

An interesting absence in these histories is any depiction of the Templars as the guardians of secret treasure or gnostic knowledge, practising magic or devil worship, surviving as Freemasons, or indeed any other stories of Templar survival, all major features of popular views of the order today. In fact, Fuller sometimes overstates the destruction of military orders, claiming that the Teutonic Knights were abolished in 1525, rather than only losing their Prussian territories and grandmaster.[65] Each of these four authors sees the Templars, though flawed, as largely innocent of the charges they faced.[66] While Ashmole was an early Freemason, he made no attempt to link his organisation with the Templars, such a connection, widespread today, was not invented until the mid-eighteenth century.[67] Though there were Templar lodges in England by 1778, the link does not seem to have made it into the mainstream of British historical consciousness until the nineteenth and twentieth centuries, as the following chapter shall show.[68]

Notes

1 The two main monographs on crusader medievalism both focus on this period and region: Elizabeth Siberry, *The New Crusaders: Images of the Crusades in the 19th and Early 20th Centuries* (Aldershot, 2000); Mike Horswell, *The Rise and Fall of British Crusader Medievalism, c. 1825–1945* (Abingdon, 2018). See also Elizabeth Siberry, 'Victorian Perceptions of the Military Orders', in Malcolm Barber (ed.), *The Military Orders: Fighting for the Faith and Caring for the Sick* (London, 1994), pp. 365–72; Adam Knobler, 'Holy Wars, Empires, and the Portability of the Past: The Modern Uses of Medieval Crusades', *Comparative Studies in Society and History*, 48:2 (April 2006), pp. 293–325; Mike Horswell and Jonathan Phillips (eds.), *Perceptions of the Crusades from the Nineteenth to the Twenty-First Century: Engaging the Crusades*, Volume One (Abingdon, 2018); Elizabeth Siberry, *Tales of the Crusaders – Remembering the Crusades in Britain: Engaging the Crusades*, Volume Six (Abingdon, 2021).

2 For example, the November 1799 cartoon *Buonaparte's Dance of Death* depicts Napoleon being 'Stabb'd at Malta!' by a figure in a green and yellow uniform with the papakha hat of a Cossack, rather than the red and white uniforms of the eighteenth-century Hospitallers: London, The British Museum, 1948,0214.648. This is unlikely to be a reference to the order's co-option by Paul I of Russia, who had himself elected grand master on 7 November 1798 as the cartoon's depiction of Egyptian and 'Tripoline' figures is equally inaccurate: H.J.A. Sire, *The Knights of Malta* (London, 1994), pp. 243–45. More likely, the cartoonist was using this imagery as a shorthand to convey a foreign nature, rather than accuracy.

3 Charles Press, 'The Georgian Political Print and Democratic Institutions', *Comparative Studies in Society and History*, 19:2 (April 1977), p. 223.

4 For example, *Nevves from Babylon* (London, 1637); *Nevves from the Great Turke* (London, 1645); 'Foreign Affairs', *Ipswich Journal*, 24 December 1720, p. 1; 'Milan, June 30', *Newcastle Courant*, 21 July 1722, p. 5; 'Paris, January 16', *Stamford Mercury*, 17 January 1723, p. 23.

5 Francis Beaumont and John Fletcher, *Comedies and Tragedies Written by Francis Beaumont and John Fletcher* (London, 1647); *The Lady of Brumpton, and Knight of Malta* (London, 1721); *The Knight of Malta: or, the Reward of Constancy* (London, 1724); George Monck Berkeley, *Heloise: or, the Siege of Rhodes*, two vols (London, 1788).

6 Christopher Tyerman, *The Debate on the Crusades* (Manchester, 2011), p. 62.

7 The first account in English was a translation of André Favyn's *Le Theatre d'Honneur et de Chevalerie* in 1623, which also catalogued the military and chivalric orders. However, it does not appear to have sold well as it was not reprinted and no further editions were produced: André Favyn, *The Theater of Honour and Knight-hood* (London, 1623).

8 James Fieser, 'Editorial Introduction', in James Fieser (ed.), *Early Responses to Hume Volume Seven: Early Responses to Hume's History of England* (Bristol, 2002), p. xxi.

9 René Aubert, abbé de Vertot, *The History of the Knights of Malta*, two vols (London, 1728).

10 W.B. Patterson, 'Fuller, Thomas', *Oxford Dictionary of National Biography* (Oxford University Press, 2004), online ed., January 2008, doi.org/10.1093/ref:odnb/10236 [accessed 15 July 2021].

11 For an overview of Fuller's place in crusade historiography, see Tyerman, *Debate on the Crusades*, pp. 60–64. For studies of his *Holy Warre* as a whole, rather than his depiction of the military orders specifically, see Bernard Hamilton, 'An Anglican View of the Crusades: Thomas Fuller's *The Historie of the Holy Warre*', in Peter D. Clarke and Charlotte Methuen (eds.), *The Church on Its Past (Studies in Church History*, Vol. 49*)* (Woodbridge, 2013), pp. 121–31, and W.B. Patterson, *Thomas Fuller: Discovering England's Religious Past* (Oxford, 2018), pp. 42–77.

12 Thomas Fuller, *The Historie of the Holy Warre* (Cambridge, 1639), pp. 47–49, 65–66, 75–76, 189–90, 193–94, 229–42, 257–58.

13 Thomas Fuller, *The Historie of the Holy Warre* (Cambridge, 1639), pp. 241–42.

14 Ibid., p. 48. Fuller is not being entirely unfair in condemning the order for failing to adhere to these ideals, at least when it comes to duelling

and neutrality in secular disputes. The Hospitallers on Malta had a strong duelling culture, while the order's officials in Europe sometimes fought in wars between Christian rulers: Emanuel Buttigieg, *Nobility, Faith and Masculinity: The Hospitaller Knights of Malta, c.1580-c.1700* (London, 2011), pp. 161–65; Helen J. Nicholson, 'Holy Warriors, Worldly War: Military Religious Orders and Secular Conflict', *Journal of Medieval Military History*, xvii (2019), pp. 61–79.

15 Fuller, *Historie of the Holy Warre*, pp. 75–76.

16 Ibid., p. 66.

17 Ibid., pp. 188–90, 193–95.

18 Ibid., p. 229.

19 Ibid., p. 234.

20 Ibid., p. 257.

21 Ibid., p. 258.

22 Ibid., pp. 234–35.

23 Ibid., p. 235.

24 Ibid., p. 236.

25 Ibid., p. 237.

26 Ibid., p. 233.

27 Ibid., pp. 282–86.

28 *A Fourme to Be Used in Common Prayer Every Wednesdaye and Fryday, within the Cittie and Dioces of London: For the Delivery of Those Christians, That Are Now Invaded by the Turk* (London, 1565); *A Shortforme of Thanksgeving for the Deliverie of the Isle of Malta from the Turkes. Set Forth by Matthew Archebyshop of Canterburye* (London, 1565).

29 Christopher Tyerman, *England and the Crusades* (London, 1988), p. 349.

30 Richard Knolle, *The Generall Historie of the Turkes* (London, 1603). For recovery treatises, see Antony Leopold, *How to Recover the Holy Land: The Crusade Proposals of the Late Thirteenth and Early Fourteenth Centuries* (Aldershot, 2000).

31 Hamilton, 'An Anglican View', p. 130.

32 Fuller, *Historie of the Holy War*, p. 242.

33 Michael Hunter, 'Ashmole, Elias', *Oxford Dictionary of National Biography* (Oxford University Press, 2004), online ed., May 2006, doi.org/10.1093/ref:odnb/764 [accessed 14 April 2021].

34 Elias Ashmole, *The Institution, Laws and Ceremonies of the Most Noble Order of the Garter* (London, 1672), pp. 48–94.

35 Ibid., p. 48.

36 Ibid., p. 83.

37 Joseph Micheli y Márquez, *Tesoro Militar de Cavallaria* (Madrid, 1642), ff. 57r-v.

38 St Birgitta's description of a dubbing ceremony for knights in her *Revelationes* could be interpreted as demonstrating that she contemplated forming a military order: Birgitta of Sweden, *The Revelations of St. Birgitta of Sweden Volume I: Liber Caelestis*, eds. Denis Searby and Bridget Morris, i (Oxford, 2006), pp. 206–208. However, this has been interpreted as at best a call for a lay fraternity of knights, not a religious one: Emilia Żochowska, 'The Christian Kingdom as an Image of the Heavenly Kingdom according to St. Birgitta of Sweden', unpublished Ph.D. thesis (University of Southern Denmark, 2010), p. 197.

39 Hans Cnattingius, 'The Order of the Knights of St. Bridget', *Annales Academiae Regiae Scientiarum Upsaliensis*, 11 (1967), pp. 10–12, 25.

40 In addition to the order of St Birgitta, these are the orders of the Holy Sepulchre, of St John of Acre (likely an early modern chivalric creation), of St Blaise, of SS Cosmas and Damian, of St Katherine of Sinai, of St Anthony in Ethiopia, the Constantinian Order of St George (an early modern chivalric order), the order of St Saviour in Aragon (perhaps a confusion with the Bridgettines), of the Wing of St Michael (an early modern chivalric order), of St Gereon, of the Holy Ghost in Rome (a religious order), of St Mary of Mercy (the Mercedarians, a religious order), of the Rosary, of the Passion of Jesus Christ (proposed but never founded), of the Holy Ghost again, of St George in Rome, of St Paul, of Pios/of the Golden Spur (a papal chivalric order), of Loretto (perhaps confused with the Loretto Sisters), of the Christian Militia (existed more in theory than reality). The Knights of the Holy Sepulchre do exist today as a chivalric order of the Catholic Church, but there is no contemporary evidence of a medieval military order by that name. Ashmole probably confused them with the genuine Canons of the Holy Sepulchre, who were non-military.

41 F.C. Woodhouse, *The Military Religious Orders of the Middle Ages: The Hospitallers, the Templars, the Teutonic Knights, and Others* (London, 1879).

42 Ashmole, *Institution, Laws and Ceremonies*, p. 55.

43 Ibid., p. 51.

44 Ibid., p. 56.

45 Ibid.

46 Ibid., p. 54.

47 Ibid., p. 83.

48 The claim that the Mercedarians were a military order originated in the sixteenth century. They actually originated as a lay confraternity which later became a religious order: James Brodman, 'The Origins of the Mercedarian Order: A Reassessment', *Studia Monastica*, 19 (1977), pp. 353–60.

49 Ashmole, *Institution, Laws and Ceremonies*, p. 79.

50 Ibid., p. 61.

51 For a biography of Hume, see Ernest C. Mossner, *The Life of David Hume* (Oxford, rev. ed., 1980).

52 Tyerman, *Debate on the Crusades*, p. 81.

53 David Hume, *The History of England from the Invasion of Julius Caesar to the Revolution in 1688*, eight vols (London, rev. ed., 1773), ii, pp. 361–62.

54 Ibid., ii, pp. 362–64.

55 Ibid., ii, p. 362.

56 Ibid., iv, p. 205.

57 John Gawthrop, 'A History of Edward Gibbon's Six Autobiographical Manuscripts', *British Library Journal*, 25 (1999), p. 194.

58 Edward Gibbon, *The History of the Decline and Fall of the Roman Empire*, six vols (London, 1776–88), vi, p. 65.

59 Gibbon, *Decline and Fall*, iii, pp. 632–33. I would like to thank Dr Colin Haydon for this point.

60 Ibid., vi, pp. 65–66.

61 Ibid., vi, p. 66.

62 Ibid., vi, pp. 314–15.

63 Ibid., i, p. 27.
64 Siberry, 'Victorian Perceptions', 369–72.
65 Fuller, *Historie of the Holy Warre*, p. 236. Ashmole correctly notes their continued survival in Germany: Ashmole, *Institution, Laws and Ceremonies*, p. 59.
66 The seventeenth and eighteenth centuries in France also saw a growing reassessment of the order's guilt: Philippe Josserand, 'The Templar Order in Public and Cultural Debate in France during the Eighteenth and Nineteenth Centuries', in Helen J. Nicholson and Jochen Burgtorf (eds.), *The Templars, the Hospitallers and the Crusades: Essays in Homage to Alan J. Forey* (Abingdon, 2020), pp. 145–46.
67 For the creation of the Templar-Freemason link, see Peter Partner, *The Knights Templar and Their Myth* (Rochester, VT, rev. ed., 1990), pp. 110–24 and Josserand 'The Templar Order', pp. 146–47.
68 Ibid., p. 116.

Bibliography

Primary

A Fourme to Be Used in Common Prayer Every Wednesdaye and Fryday, within the Cittie and Dioces of London: For the Delivery of those Christians, that Are Now Invaded by the Turk. London, 1565.

A Shortforme of Thanksgeving for the Deliverie of the Isle of Malta from the Turkes. Set Forth by Matthew Archebyshop of Canterburye. London: William Seres, 1565.

Beaumont, Francis and John Fletcher. *Comedies and Tragedies Written by Francis Beaumont and John Fletcher*. London: Humphrey Moseley and Humphrey Robinson, 1647.

Berkeley, George Monck. *Heloise: Or, The Siege of Rhodes*. two vols, London: J. Forbes, C. Elliot, T. Kay, P. McQueen, T. and J. Egerton, Shepperdston and Reynold, C. Stalker, 1788.

Ipswich Journal, 24 December 1720.

London, The British Museum. 1948,0214.648.

Nevves from Babylon. London: T. Harper, 1637.

Nevves from the Great Turke. London: Jo. Handcock, 1645.

Newcastle Courant, 21 July 1722.

The Knight of Malta: or, the Reward of Constancy. London: T. Corbett, 1724.

The Lady of Brumpton, and Knight of Malta. London: J. Roberts, 1721.

Stamford Mercury, 17 January 1723.

Secondary

Ashmole, Elias. *The Institution, Laws and Ceremonies of the Most Noble Order of the Garter*. London: J. Macock, 1672.

Aubert, René, abbé de Vertot. *The History of the Knights of Malta.* two vols. London: G. Strahan, 1728.

Barber, Malcolm (ed.). *The Military Orders: Fighting for the Faith and Caring for the Sick.* London: Ashgate, 1994.

Birgitta of Sweden. *The Revelations of St. Birgitta of Sweden Volume I: Liber Caelestis.* eds. Denis Searby and Bridget Morris. Oxford: Oxford University Press, 2006.

Brodman, James. 'The Origins of the Mercedarian Order: A Reassessment'. *Studia Monastica*, 19 (1977), pp. 353–60.

Buttigieg, Emanuel. *Nobility, Faith and Masculinity: The Hospitaller Knights of Malta, c.1580–c.1700.* London: Continuum, 2011.

Clarke, Peter D. and Charlotte Methuen (eds.). *The Church on Its Past* (Studies in Church History, Vol. 49). Woodbridge: Boydell, 2013.

Cnattingius, Hans. 'The Order of the Knights of St. Bridget'. *Annales Academiae Regiae Scientiarum Upsaliensis*, 11 (1967), pp. 5–35.

Favyn, André. *The Theater of Honour and Knight-hood.* London: William Iaggard, 1623.

Fieser, James (ed.). *Early Responses to Hume Volume Seven: Early Responses to Hume's History of England.* Bristol: Bloomsbury, 2002.

Fuller, Thomas. *The Historie of the Holy Warre.* Cambridge: Thomas Buck, 1639.

Gawthrop, John. 'A History of Edward Gibbon's Six Autobiographical Manuscripts'. *British Library Journal*, 25 (1999), pp. 188–203.

Gibbon, Edward. *The History of the Decline and Fall of the Roman Empire.* six vols. London: W. Strahan and T. Cadell, 1776–88.

Horswell, Mike. *The Rise and Fall of British Crusader Medievalism, c. 1825–1945.* Abingdon: Routledge, 2018.

Horswell, Mike and Jonathan Phillips (eds.). *Perceptions of the Crusades from the Nineteenth to the Twenty-First Century: Engaging the Crusades*, Volume One. Abingdon: Routledge, 2018.

Hume, David. *The History of England from the Invasion of Julius Caesar to the Revolution in 1688.* eight vols. London: T. Cadell, rev. ed., 1773.

Hunter, Michael. 'Ashmole, Elias'. *Oxford Dictionary of National Biography* (Oxford University Press, 2004). online ed., May 2006, doi.org/10.1093/ref:odnb/764 [accessed 14 April 2021].

Knobler, Adam. 'Holy Wars, Empires, and the Portability of the Past: The Modern Uses of Medieval Crusades'. *Comparative Studies in Society and History*, 48:2 (April 2006), pp. 293–325.

Knolle, Richard. *The Generall Historie of the Turkes.* London: Adam Islip, 1603.

Leopold, Antony. *How to Recover the Holy Land: The Crusade Proposals of the Late Thirteenth and Early Fourteenth Centuries.* Aldershot: Ashgate, 2000.

Micheli y Márquez, Joseph. *Tesoro Militar de Cavallaria.* Madrid: Moreno Gargallo, 1642.

Mossner, Ernest C. *The Life of David Hume.* Oxford: Oxford University Press, rev. ed., 1980.

Nicholson, Helen J. 'Holy Warriors, Worldly War: Military Religious Orders and Secular Conflict'. *Journal of Medieval Military History*, xvii (2019), pp. 61–79.

Nicholson, Helen J. and Jochen Burgtorf (eds.). *The Templars, the Hospitallers and the Crusades: Essays in Homage to Alan J. Forey.* Abingdon: Routledge, 2020.

Partner, Peter. *The Knights Templar and their Myth.* Rochester, VT: Destiny Books, rev. ed., 1990.

Patterson, W.B. 'Fuller, Thomas'. *Oxford Dictionary of National Biography* (Oxford University Press, 2004). online ed., January 2008, doi.org/10.1093/ref:odnb/10236 [accessed 15 July 2021].

———. *Thomas Fuller: Discovering England's Religious Past.* Oxford: Oxford University Press, 2018.

Press, Charles. 'The Georgian Political Print and Democratic Institutions'. *Comparative Studies in Society and History*, 19:2 (April 1977), pp. 216–38.

Siberry, Elizabeth. *The New Crusaders: Images of the Crusades in the 19th and Early 20th Centuries.* Aldershot: Ashgate, 2000.

———. *Tales of the Crusaders – Remembering the Crusades in Britain: Engaging the Crusades*, Volume Six. Abingdon: Routledge, 2021.

Sire, H.J.A. *The Knights of Malta.* London: Yale University Press, 1994.

Tyerman, Christopher. *England and the Crusades.* London: University of Chicago Press, 1988.

———. *The Debate on the Crusades.* Manchester: Manchester University Press, 2011.

Woodhouse, F.C. *The Military Religious Orders of the Middle Ages: The Hospitallers, the Templars, the Teutonic Knights, and Others.* London: Society for Promoting Christian Knowledge, 1879.

Żochowska, Emilia. 'The Christian Kingdom as an Image of the Heavenly Kingdom according to St. Birgitta of Sweden'. Unpublished Ph.D. thesis (University of Southern Denmark, 2010).

2 Rosslyn Chapel

Templar Pseudo-history, 'Symbology', and the Far-right

Lizzie Swarbrick

Rosslyn Chapel is perhaps the most infamous medieval church in the British Isles. Its idiosyncratic appearance has been explained as the product of ancient alien Atlanteans, interdimensional portals, pagan practices, early Freemasonry, covert Templar activity, and many other fantastic things besides. None of this is true. Reinterpreting Rosslyn has a long history, stretching back until the early seventeenth century. The number and persistence of pseudo-histories surrounding Rosslyn has made it a playground for conspiracy theorists. These erroneous ideas about the chapel are often based on theorists' attempts to interpret the huge number of images which adorn this church – a kind of pseudo-art-history. Michael Baigent and Richard Leigh even describe Rosslyn as 'a petrified compendium of esoterica'.[1] People often dismiss legends about the church as idle fantasies, but some have ended up as fake foundational histories for repugnant twenty-first-century political ideologies. In this chapter I trace the history of reinterpreting Rosslyn as a Templar building, examine various aspects of the chapel which have been misidentified as Templar, and show the dangerous consequences of these false ideas.

The Real Rosslyn Chapel

First, the facts of the matter. Rosslyn Chapel, more properly known as the collegiate church of St Matthew in Roslin, was founded by Sir William Sinclair around 1450, and the building begun before 1447 (Figure 2.1).[2] Collegiate churches were simply organisations in which more than one clergyman worked together in praise of God and for the salvation of certain persons' souls. They were not necessarily educational (though medieval universities grew out of them). Forty-nine were founded in Scotland between 1250 and 1546.[3] Founding a collegiate

DOI: 10.4324/9781003200802-3

Figure 2.1 Rosslyn Chapel exterior, from the south east. © Lizzie Swarbrick.

church was an ambitious and expensive project, but it was not unusual in late medieval Scotland.

Founding Rosslyn was an act of charity by William Sinclair, because it ensured that a group of clergy would sing in perpetuity, giving glory to god. The prayers offered there on his and his family's behalf also worked to shorten their time in Purgatory. The magnificence of the building at Rosslyn formed part of this act of charity, because all money spent on the church was conceived as a 'happy commerce', transferring worldly goods into spiritual credit.[4] The church overlooks Roslin Glen and the Sinclair's castle. Together, these buildings and the landscape around them became statements of worldly authority and good taste. The bombastic architecture and decoration at Rosslyn Chapel also fulfilled these purposes: charitable, worshipful, salvific, and propagandistic. All of this is to say that the reasons behind founding and building Rosslyn are not secret, nor were they strange in the context of late medieval lordship and piety.

Rosslyn is famous for its sculptures, and it is right to say that this wealth of imagery is extraordinary. In Scotland, most sacred images

Figure 2.2 Extraordinary compressed sculptures. Rosslyn Chapel interior, south east corner. © Lizzie Swarbrick/Rosslyn Chapel Trust.

were destroyed during the Reformation. This is true also at Rosslyn; however, here a huge number of marginal images survive. The vast majority are conventional, but there are so many packed into a relatively small space that their combinations can seem strange (Figure 2.2). Contrary to popular belief, there are a huge number of sculptures of Christian figures and narratives. It is also important to say that foliate heads (the so-called Green Men), all manner of animals, mischievous figures, and skeletons were also common in late medieval churches. Playfulness and even profanity are to be expected.

That said, there are a few idiosyncratic aspects of Rosslyn: the sheer level of surface ornament, the spatial order of some images, and some individual sculptures. This is certainly not a bible in stone, it would be completely useless as a didactic tool. Instead, it is a set of complex prompts to aid contemplation for its culturally sophisticated patron, Sir William Sinclair. Rosslyn is testament to the creative milieu of late medieval Scotland. No original image in the chapel exists outwith this context. There are no secret codes to crack.

Rosslyn's physical history has a great bearing on how it is perceived. Begun before 1447, the church building was left unfinished after the founder died c.1480. In the Middle Ages it was common for building projects to extend beyond one generation, and in this case William's son Oliver simply did not have the funds to carry on.[5] Only the chancel and parts of the transepts were ever fully built, and the nave was never completed beyond its foundations. Rosslyn worked much like any other collegiate church and survived the effects of the Reformation until 1591–92 when the then Sinclair lord was forced to demolish the images and altars.[6] After this, the church was abandoned.

What followed was a complicated history of destruction, ruination, and invasive repair. Rosslyn suffered from some iconoclasm, and natural weathering resulted in significant damage. Three major restorations transformed the appearance of the church. The first, by John Baxter in 1736, was so bad that the Sinclair patron asked to be forgiven his 'folly of ever having meddled with it [the church]'.[7] The second was by William Burn (1837–45) and the third by David Bryce (1860). Bryce's work was particularly controversial – he recut or replaced numerous sculptures – and was condemned by prominent antiquarians.[8] The church was still suffering from damp, so, in 1954, in a misguided attempt to deal with it, the Ministry of Works scoured the church with wire brushes and an ammonia wash, grouted gaps in sculpture, and sprayed the entire interior in cementitious slurry.[9] The current Earl and Countess of Rosslyn oversaw a thorough conservation of the chapel. This last episode means that the church now looks in such good condition that casual visitors may never be aware of Rosslyn's calamitous history.

Each of these interventions in the building at Rosslyn were well-meaning in their time, but cumulatively they have muddied the picture. It is completely unclear to the untrained eye which parts of the church are original, which are restored, and the thick cement coating disguises masonry breaks and even the subjects of several carvings. This double loss – of medieval fabric and of clarity about what remains – is the most significant factor which has led to misinterpretations of Rosslyn Chapel.

Interpretive History – Forgetting, Freemasonry, and Templarism

Running alongside this physical history is a long tradition of reimagining Rosslyn. To begin, the Reformation was a cataclysm for both the physical church and the understanding of its meaning. The repercussions of iconoclasm, in terms of how people understood what remained, were huge. This is still felt in the ignorance of commonplace medieval images. Without this disjuncture, none of the subsequent misinterpretations could exist.

The next key event was the emergence of Speculative Freemasonry. Freemasons in the modern sense are separate from operative masons, i.e. guilds or lodges of actual working masons. Freemasonry did not exist when Rosslyn was built, but the emergent Grand Lodge of Scotland was keen to claim an imagined noble ancestry. It was for this reason that in 1600/1601 and 1627/1628, Freemasonic lodges wrote to two successive lords of Roslin (both called William Sinclair) asking each to be the first Grand Master: claiming that their family 'hes for ever bene patrones and p[ro]tectoris of ws and our previleges'.[10] There is no evidence that the Sinclairs ever had links to Freemasons before the seventeenth century. Stevenson, the expert in early Scottish Freemasonry, concludes that claims of destroyed documents which allegedly proved earlier links were invented.[11] Stevenson does suggest that the magnificence of Rosslyn Chapel could be thought of as evidence in and of itself, but by that logic, the Cistercian monks at Melrose could also be closet Grand Masters.[12] It is through these fabricated Masonic ties that Rosslyn gained its false Templar attribution.

Freemasonry incorporated elements of Renaissance esotericism, and in the mid-eighteenth century these ideas took on a more ambitious and Gothic tone.[13] In 1736 Chevalier Ramsay gave a lecture to noble Scottish Freemasons living in France in which he invented a romantic knightly origin for their organisation.[14] In the 1760s a self-styled Scottish nobleman called George Frederick Johnson claimed that the antecedents of the Freemasons were not humble stoneworkers, but were in fact the Knights Templar.[15] Johnson claimed he had access to lost Templar secrets, including the whereabouts of buried treasure.[16] There is no truth in any of this, and Peter Partner bluntly describes this eighteenth-century birth of Templarism as 'a belief manufactured by charlatans for their dupes'.[17] The spurious claim that the Sinclairs had been patrons of Freemasons, when put together with the invention of Freemasonic Templarism, was enough to make people believe that Rosslyn Chapel was a Templar church. In short, it is this point, in the mid-eighteenth century, that the perception of Rosslyn as Templar first emerged. It is also worth noting that this eighteenth-century invention of Templarism establishes many of the main features of Templar pseudo-histories which are still alive today: nostalgia for a masculine spiritual-fraternal organisation, self-perceived victimhood, and interest in treasure and fame.

All of this might have remained an esoteric curiosity, had the chapel not itself become famous. Through the nineteenth century, Rosslyn Chapel became an important place for Romantic poets and artists. Its ruined state and its position atop a pleasant, wooded glen made it an ideal place for people to get a taste of Scottish wildness, without actually having to venture very far from Edinburgh. With the advent of train travel, Rosslyn was opened up to many more tourists, and coaches regularly ran from Waverley station. One guide from 1852 mentions its popularity amongst picnickers and takes a rather sarcastic tone, mentioning that 'the usual fables [...] are duly narrated to the visitor'.[18]

Within this period, Rosslyn was celebrated specifically because of its romantic state of disrepair. William Wordsworth's poem *Composed in Roslin Chapel during a Storm* plays upon the idea of ruined and rediscovered spirituality. He describes Rosslyn Chapel as a 'Temple', making it seem like the place is for some forgotten pagan nature-worship, or possibly a Freemasonic lodge. This idea of indistinct spiritual experience within the crumbling building creates a potent sense of something significant as having been lost – forgotten or suppressed. It also distances Rosslyn from its context of having been a fairly ordinary working medieval church, instead it becomes a kind of natural spring of strange spirituality.

Jacques-Louis Mandé Daguerre's painting *Interior of Roslin Chapel* (1824, Musée des Beaux-Arts, Rouen) (Figure 2.3) is particularly important for our purposes. Here, the shadowy interior has been inflated to cathedral-like proportions. Only upon looking closely is it possible to see that two of the tiny figures' cloaks open to reveal that underneath they are garbed in white, with a red cross on their chests, the dress of Templars. They direct the work of two people who are lifting stone flags. In their clandestine excavation, a bone and a box are barely visible. As the viewer, you are forced to search for this scene within the large, dim interior, and to see what they might be uncovering, you must really peer in. The viewer's motions thus reflect those of the painted figures, both have to delve to see what is there. The important thing is that you, the viewer, become involved in these actions. Within this one painting are a number of threads which make up Rosslyn's place within Templar pseudo-history. You have the idea of a great secret at Rosslyn, the potential for real buried treasure, the sense that the truth can be uncovered by the right people, and the active inclusion of the audience.

These ideas about Rosslyn grew exponentially in the twentieth century. Rosslyn seems to attract all sorts of ideas: psychic energies, ghosts, ancient aliens, space travel, ley lines and Reshel grids, even conspiracy theories about Elvis Presley's death. Many of these theories stray into the territory of ideas about a New World Order or the Illuminati. The Templars frequently feature, usually as a group battling against hegemonic persecutors. What runs throughout all these

Figure 2.3 Jacques-Louis Mandé Daguerre, Interior of Roslin Chapel (1824, Musée des Beaux-Arts, Rouen), Wikimedia Commons.

fantastical narratives is the idea that a secret treasure – be that material goods or information – is contained within Rosslyn, hidden away from mainstream oppressors, that an elect group of people who truly understand can uncover it, and that you are invited to join the quest.

In the 1980s, pseudo-historical Templar narratives concerning Rosslyn Chapel really flourished. Rosslyn only plays a bit part in *The Holy Blood and the Holy Grail*, but that book spawned an enormous corpus of writing, and, within many, Rosslyn takes centre stage.[19] The most entertaining is *Batman: The Scottish Connection*, where Batman discovers the treasures of the Temple of Jerusalem in the crypt at Rosslyn Chapel.[20] This secret vault is accessed by twisting one of Rosslyn's enigmatic 'Green Men' sculptures.[21] Of course the most famous is Dan Brown's *The Da Vinci Code*, which culminates with the discovery of the secret of the Sangreal at Rosslyn.[22] Brown introduces the church as follows:

> Rosslyn Chapel – often called the Cathedral of Codes – stands seven miles south of Edinburgh, on the site of an ancient Mithraic temple. Built by the Knights Templar in 1446, the chapel is engraved with a mind-boggling array of symbols from the Jewish, Christian, Egyptian, Masonic and pagan traditions.[23]

Here Brown uses many aspects of Rosslyn's interpretive history which I have explored so far, particularly the idea of the site as a natural spring of esoteric spirituality.

The legend of Templars fleeing to Scotland and to Rosslyn after their dissolution has spread to the extent to which the 2017 official book about the chapel begins recounting it by saying 'at this point it is well documented that...'.[24] It is incorrect, but almost endlessly repeated. Alongside the aforementioned blockbusters are a seemingly infinite number of Rosslyn Templar focused books, magazine articles, documentaries, tourist guide entries, pamphlets, blogs, YouTube videos, memes, social media posts, and all the unquantifiable, informal, orally transmitted storytelling. Through all these many means pseudo-histories are transmitted by people who are genuinely excited to have a part in uncovering secrets at Rosslyn.

Within this raucous world of intersecting theories are people who wish to use Rosslyn Chapel for their own ends: the racist far-right. Various aspects of Rosslyn are included in their myth-making (for example, the fake story about the so-called 'Indian corn' in the church), but the images and ideas they use are generally directly Templar.[25] In this way, Rosslyn is co-opted into a much broader misuse of Crusader and Templar imagery by white supremacist and far-right groups. This phenomenon is as ubiquitous as it is dangerous.[26] Templar flags (most simply a red cross on a white background, though there are multiple different versions) were flown at Charlottesville, by Trump supporters during the failed insurrection on the U.S. Capitol in January 2021, and at other events attended by the far-right such as the COVID-19 anti-lockdown protests.[27] Perhaps the most deplorable example is the mass murderer Anders Behring Breivik, who claimed he was acting as a Templar knight when he killed 77 people in Oslo.[28]

People who claim links to Templars often do so only on a superficial level.[29] Wollenberg notes that Breivik does not attempt to claim real continuity with the Templars, and only 'uses their name, history, and symbology'.[30] It is this 'symbology' which is the focus of the rest of this chapter. There is no doubt that medieval art and architecture are important tools for white nationalists. Images function as easily shareable shortcuts to manufacture historicity, and are used to provoke and recruit people. Rosslyn is specifically used by the actively fascist and Islamophobic group Knights Templar Order International (KTI).[31] As with other organisations' uses of medieval imagery, Rosslyn Chapel is used to add fake authenticity, and the KTI also borrow from Rosslyn's popularity. This is returned to in detail below. The adoption of Templar and Rosslyn pseudo-history and imagery by the far-right carries on the themes seen earlier in this chapter: again we have a kind of esoteric cosplay, claims of victimhood, and the intended activation of whoever consumes this media to join what they see as a crusade.

Cracking the Codes

Pseudo-historians show a marked preference for using material and visual culture as evidence for a number of reasons. First, buildings, artefacts, objects, and works of art are physically solid, and this lends them the quality of being perceived as figuratively substantial pieces of evidence. Amateurs often treat material culture as if it is less susceptible to bias or forgery than documents, as if their materials, patina, survival, and presentation imbue them with automatic authenticity. So, Rosslyn Chapel and, by extension, the interpretive framework of signs and leaflets there are afforded the utmost trust. They are the literal and figurative cornerstones of pseudo-histories.

Photographs reproduce part of this tangible quality and confer a sense of solidity to books which include them. A striking number of popular conspiracy books on Rosslyn have chunky plate sections. Bestsellers such as *Holy Blood Holy Grail* and *The Da Vinci Code* even have illustrated special reissues, creating hardback tomes which are physically little different from academic books. In this way, sculptures at Rosslyn Chapel play a crucial role in Templar pseudo-histories, by providing them with substantial, though entirely invented, evidence.

Second, material culture communicates ideas and narratives in distinctive ways. Tim Wallace Murphy described the images at Rosslyn as a 'puzzle [...] being taught in the old-fashioned way'.[32] *The Da Vinci Code* similarly discusses images, artefacts, and buildings as if they are a more natural and direct form of communication than writing. At one point Robert Langdon and Sophie Neveu ponder the survival of the grail story. Langdon explains that 'the Church outlawed' it, but that it was passed on through 'discrete channels... channels that supported metaphor and symbolism', to which Neveu replies: 'Of course. The arts'.[33] Later, Dan Brown describes Rosslyn as '*Symbology heaven*'.[34] So, the inference is that the sculptures at Rosslyn would be a perfectly legible set of instructions to help us find the truth, if only the knowledge had not been purposefully suppressed. Crucially, pseudo-histories claim to reveal this secret 'symbology', and then invite their audience apply these strange and superficial methods to images they may see.

In real life, art, buildings, and artefacts have expressive, context-dependent, and slippery meanings. They are far from being innately or automatically understood. This openness is the very thing pseudo-art-historians exploit when they invent unfounded interpretations, even if they still present images as solidly and instinctively understandable. The language of 'symbology' is also revealing, with images regularly described as 'symbols', 'puzzles', or 'codes'. This language reduces the complexity and power of images until they are mere ciphers, where x simply stands for y. It also involves the audience. Presenting a work of art as a puzzle or a code offers the reader a chance to become a cryptographer. I have seen many visitors at Rosslyn applying Robert Langdon-like logic to sculptures not referenced by Dan Brown. Like the viewer of Daguerre's painting, the reader is encouraged to join in to 'solve the mystery, break the code, seek the truth'.[35]

Cornerstones

In the north-west of Rosslyn Chapel, there is a small funerary monument (Figure 2.4) with a carving of a sword, an eight-pointed floriated cross, and the following inscription:

+ WILLH'M DE SINNCL ER

Andrew Sinclair uses an image of this for the cover of his popular pseudo-historical book *The Sword and the Grail*.[36] In the preface, entitled 'A Quest', Sinclair describes this stone as if it were a great personal find, and one which he claims links Rosslyn to the Templars and the pre-Columbian settlement of North America.[37] He states: 'this discovery is the cornerstone of this book'.[38]

There are a number of issues here. First, the iconography is commonplace on medieval grave markers, and has no links to military orders. Second, the way the text is awkwardly incorporated shows that

Figure 2.4 Altered medieval graveslab purported to commemorate William Sinclair, with modern plinth describing him as a Knight Templar. North aisle, Rosslyn Chapel. © Lizzie Swarbrick / Rosslyn Chapel Trust.

it is a later addition. There is no evidence that this is the monument for a Sinclair lord, and it would be unusual for a senior nobleman to be buried with such a small and simple marker. So, it is not a Templar gravestone and it probably never commemorated a Sinclair lord. This is the falsified and misinterpreted evidential cornerstone for a variety of Templar theories.

Its presentation within the chapel pushes unwary viewers towards this incorrect interpretation, because it is now shown on top of a modern plinth bearing the inscription:

WILLIAM DE St. CLAIR
KNIGHT TEMPLAR

A Google image search for 'Rosslyn Chapel Knights Templar' turns up many results with an image of this graveslab and its plinth. It is clear from captions that viewers are often unaware that the plinth is modern. For example, Robert Lomas, the writer who was supposedly the inspiration for Dan Brown's 'symbologist' Robert Langdon, captions a photo of this with: 'The Tombstone of the Templar William St Clair, preserved in Rosslyn'.[39] The re-presentation of the graveslab on the modern base with its misleading inscription compounds the effect of the earlier alteration of this grave marker. As such, its appearance within the controlled and presumed-authentic space of the chapel interior provides apparently real physical evidence for those seeking Templar artefacts.

A second supposedly Templar sculpture at Rosslyn can be found on a corbel for a statue in the jamb of a window in the south aisle. The sculpture (Figure 2.5) depicts two human figures: one wears mail and rides a horse, whilst the figure in the background holds aloft a cross shape. This has been misinterpreted as a depiction of a Templar knight or the seal of the Templar order, which consisted of two knights riding the same horse. Andrew Sinclair writes 'an actual carving of

Figure 2.5 St George. Purported to be a sculpture of the Templar seal. South aisle, Rosslyn Chapel. © Lizzie Swarbrick / Rosslyn Chapel Trust.

a mailed Templar knight with his lance also graces Rosslyn Chapel', before describing the corbel.[40] Robert Ferguson uses this image as the cover for his book *The Knights Templar and Scotland*, to create a strong link between the church, this imagery, and the Templars.[41] In this way, Rosslyn is misappropriated not only to provide 'evidence' for pseudo-historians but also to sell these theories to the general public.

Importantly, this sculpture is not medieval, and was probably installed under David Bryce's restoration. Nor does it depict the Templar seal. On proper examination it is clear that there is only one figure on the horse, with the other figure behind, also, only one of the figures is in armour. So, it absolutely cannot represent the Templar seal. The idea that it represents a Templar knight is just unnecessary: very few medieval people who wore armour were in military orders.

Alternative interpretations of this image abound, but the most logical explanation is that there was originally an image of St George here, which has become slightly lost in translation when replaced in the 1860s.[42] A key indication that St George was its original subject is the imagery of its pair at the other side of the window. This has been understood in wildly different ways, but knowledge of medieval iconography unequivocally reveals it to be the Annunciation. St George

Figure 2.6 Agnus Dei. Allegedly a Templar symbol. North aisle, Rosslyn Chapel. © Lizzie Swarbrick / Rosslyn Chapel Trust.

was widely venerated across medieval Europe, was understood as the perfect Christian knight, and was commonly included as an attendant to the Virgin Mary.[43] So, here in the south aisle is not a mysterious Templar seal, but a Victorian attempt to copy an image of a popular saint.

To my knowledge, I am the first to identify the Annunciation at Rosslyn, and it led me to wonder just how thoroughly medieval iconography has been forgotten. The final two examples are considered together, and further illustrate this sort of confusion. The first is in the north aisle, just above the capital of a respond marking a bay division (Figure 2.6). Here two angels emerge from a cloud and hold the *agnus Dei*: an image of the lamb of God with the cross pennant. This is widely described as another Templar symbol. For example, an image of this is captioned as 'a representation of the Knights Templar emblem' in the book *Rosslyn Chapel Decoded*.[44] Another sculpture in the north aisle, this time just west of the door, allegedly depicts the burning at the stake of Jacques de Molay, last Grand Master of the Templar Order (Figure 2.7). This dubious interpretation is regularly

Figure 2.7 Crucifixion. Claimed to be a sculpture of the death of Jacques de Molay. North aisle, Rosslyn Chapel. © Lizzie Swarbrick / Rosslyn Chapel Trust.

mentioned by guides at the church and is included in Snow's *A Rosslyn Treasury*.[45] The implication from both guides and Snow is that people who consider themselves in-the-know understand that this is a coded representation of what they see as a Templar martyrdom.

In fact, these are amongst the best-known Christian images. Of course, the *agnus Dei* is just that, an image of the lamb of God, a symbol of the resurrected Christ, drawing from imagery in St John's Gospel and the Book of Revelation. It is an extremely common medieval image, and absolutely not exclusively Templar. The second image is yet more ubiquitous: it depicts the Crucifixion of Christ. Admittedly, the figures are squashed to fit the available space, it has suffered from damage and from the 1954 sloppy cement coating, so it might not be immediately legible. Regardless, there is no indication whatsoever that this is an image of Jacques de Molay, no flames of his execution pyre, no Templar references, nothing. There is clearly a deep confusion about these images. I believe this is born from, first, an ignorance of Christian iconography as a result of Reformation iconoclasm, and, second, the exposure to it solely from within Templar pseudo-histories. Naturally, as a Christian organisation, the Templar order used Christian iconography. The error comes when people look back on medieval art solely through that lens and then see Templar symbols everywhere.

None of the images examined here are unexpected in the context of a fifteenth-century Scottish collegiate church. They need no extra justification for their existence in Rosslyn nor complex explanation of their symbolism. Still, each sculpture here is used as false evidence for conspiracy theories.

'Evidence' and Effect

As mentioned earlier, far-right groups have a long history of appropriating the history and imagery of Crusaders and Templars. Some make specific links to the sorts of pseudo-histories this chapter is concerned with. One website utilises images of pseudo-architectural geometric figures and a Templar knight superimposed on sepia historicised photos of Rosslyn Chapel. The meandering wall of text which these images accompany quotes from pop pseudo-historical books such as *Rosslyn: Guardian of the Secrets of the Holy Grail* and the bestselling *Da Vinci Code* explainer: *Secrets of the Code*.[46] In the rest of the text, the author makes a staggering range of claims about Rosslyn, centring around the idea that

> Lucifer does indeed have a Church dedicated to him here on earth. It is Rosslyn Chapel, and those who know what they're looking for within its stone-encoded walls will come to know him.[47]

Through superficial description and wild misinterpretation of Rosslyn Chapel's sculptures, the author links Rosslyn to ideas about prominent members of UK society, including the royal family, engaging in ritual paedophilia and cannibalism. This is a version of the antisemitic trope of the blood libel, the false accusation of Jewish ritual child murder, which has also arisen in theories promulgated by QAnon and as part of Pizzagate. The author further claims Rosslyn is central to attempts to bring the world under Jewish-Pagan-Satanist control, another antisemitic conspiracy. This idea can be also seen in posts on the Neo-Nazi Stormfront website and *Terrorism and the Illuminati* by David Livingstone, in which the author uses Rosslyn's 'occult symbolism' to help claim that the Sinclair family were 'secret Jews' and Templars whose red hair marked them out as being 'Luciferian', and who later 'intermarried' with the Rothschilds.[48] Though these theories are clearly very strange indeed, they demonstrate a direct link between popular conspiracy theory books, pseudo-art-history, and extremist politics.

The group calling themselves Knights Templar Order International have significantly more real-world reach.[49] Alongside appropriating more generalised Templar or Crusader imagery, the organisation specifically appropriate the pseudo-history of Rosslyn to borrow its popular appear and to provide false historicity and authenticity. The ruling body of this organisation call themselves the 'Rosslyn Priory', a website and the company name within which KTI financially operates are both called 'The Rosslyn Portal', and the reproduction Templar items which they sell go under the name 'Rosslyn Regalia'.[50] Historical replicas play a significant role in creating the sense that the KTI are a genuine continuation of medieval practices and a real-world physical force. The 'Full Knight & Regalia Package' includes a 'Unique MEMBERSHIP parchment scroll of Authenticity sent straight from the Roslyn [sic] Priory!'.[51] The cheaper, 'affiliate membership pack' includes a 'parchement' [sic] which is a poor homage to medieval manuscripts, with a historiated initial and decorative border.[52] The fact that membership is only guaranteed by the purchase of these physical items shows the important role that material culture plays in making KTI members and followers feel like they are an authentically medieval real-world community and genuine threat to their enemies.

The income generated by these sales goes towards the KTI's activities equipping people intent on actual violence against refugees and migrants, particularly Muslims, and specifically through trips to Bulgaria, Hungary, and Serbia.[53] Photos show Jim Dowson (leader of the KTI, former member of the Orange Order, the British National Party (BNP), and former leader of Britain First) with Nick Griffin (former leader of the BNP), delivering military-style bullet proof vests, communication equipment, and white gloves with red Templar crosses on them to militias in Kosovo.[54] Images of this have been carefully stage-managed to act as a recruitment tool. Dowson shared a *Daily Record* front page leading with the image and the headline 'FASCISM.. IN THE NAME OF CHRIST' on Twitter with the comment 'Up the Patriots!!', clearly relishing the press coverage of these events.[55] The combination of modern military equipment and fake Templar garb by members of the KTI's 'Rosslyn Priory' is the sharp end of the stick when it comes to the far-right's use of medieval material culture.

Conclusion

Though the KTI expressly stand in opposition to Freemasonry, the history of modern Templarism is entirely the product of eighteenth-century Masonic inventions of fake chivalric antecedents.[56] The KTI's use of the name of Rosslyn has also not occurred in a vacuum, but instead is part of a centuries-old history of people reinterpreting the spectacular sculptures at Rosslyn Chapel to support their own worldviews. The suppression of the Templars provided a gap within which pseudo-histories could grow, and the same is true at Rosslyn Chapel, where damage and restoration have made wild reinterpretation possible. It is this absence of evidence and forgetting of the real meaning of what is still there, which is the leitmotif running throughout Rosslyn Templar conspiracy theories. The modern white supremacist appropriation of Rosslyn is only made possible through these long and intertwined interpretive and physical histories.

Rosslyn Chapel is actively being used by far-right racists. They have fixed upon Rosslyn's sculptures in order to add false authenticity to their historicist claims, and the pseudo-historical fame of Rosslyn has allowed them to co-opt the church to help sell their dangerous ideologies. Popular writing about Rosslyn today still repeats conspiracy theories, and academic research tends to dismiss or simply ignore them. This is not enough. Anyone involved in Rosslyn Chapel – academic, heritage professional, guidebook writer, tour guide, and so on – we all have a duty. We must not casually dismiss pseudo-histories, but instead engage with them. We can make clear what is real history and what is fake, what is medieval and what is modern, what sculptures really meant, and how dangerous fake 'symbology' can be. Most importantly, like Daguerre's painting and the pseudo-historical entreaties to 'seek the truth', we should actively include anyone encountering our work. When faced with racist and fascist ideas, it is important to shake off our academic distance, and instead invite our audiences to discover, think, and teach with us, even, or perhaps especially, if it feels a bit tacky. Working together, we can remove the cornerstones of fake evidence from the racist far-right. This is our quest.

Notes

1 Michael Baigent and Richard Leigh, *The Temple and the Lodge* (London, 1988, 1990 reprint), p. 158.
2 There was no set spelling in the Middle Ages. I have used the family's preferred 'Rosslyn' to refer to the church, and 'Roslin' when talking about the barony, village, glen, or castle. The designation 'chapel' is also a modern change, given that it was founded as a church. For further details on the factual medieval history of the church, see Lizzie Swarbrick, 'The Medieval Art and Architecture of Scottish Collegiate Churches', unpublished PhD thesis, University of St Andrews, 2017, especially pp. 514–19.
3 Ibid.
4 *Calendar of Scottish Supplications to Rome: vol.vi, 1471–92*, eds. Alan Macquarrie, Roland Tanner, and Annie Dunlop (Edinburgh, 2017), p. 432.
5 Barbara Crawford, 'Earl William Sinclair and the Building of Roslin Collegiate Church', in ed. John Higgitt, *Medieval Art and Architecture in the Diocese of St Andrews* (Leeds, 1994), p. 106.
6 See *The Records of the Synod of Lothian and Tweeddale 1589–96, 1640–49*, ed. James Kirk (Edinburgh, 1977), pp. 21–22, 31, for the orders to destroy the altars and images.
7 A series of letters in the National Records of Scotland (NRS) to St John Clerk from Colonel James Sinclair about the church show increasing disquiet about the work Baxter undertook. See NRS GD18/5010 especially /2, /4, /6, /8. The quote is from NRS GD18/5010/4.
8 See Angelo Maggi, 'The Unmaking of Pictorial Beauty: David Roberts and the Restoration Controversy', in eds. Helen Rosslyn and Angelo Maggi, *Rosslyn Chapel: Country of Painter and Poet* (Edinburgh, 2002), pp. 51–54, 61–65. Some of the altered portions are flagged up in Christopher Wilson in Colin McWilliam, *Buildings of Scotland: Lothian except Edinburgh* (Harmondsworth, 1978, reprint 1980), p. 416.
9 The Earl and Countess of Rosslyn, *Rosslyn Chapel* (London, 2017), p. 123.
10 David Stevenson, *The Origins of Freemasonry: Scotland's Century 1590–1710* (Cambridge, 1988), p. 52.
11 Ibid, p. 58.
12 Ibid, p. 54.
13 See ibid, Chapter 5.
14 Peter Partner, *The Murdered Magicians: the Templars and their Myth* (Oxford, 1982), pp. 103–105.
15 Ibid, pp. 110–12.
16 Ibid.

17 Ibid, p. 112.
18 John Menzies, *Menzies' Scottish Tourist's Pocket Guide* (Edinburgh, 1852), pp. 183–88.
19 Michael Baigent, Richard Leigh, and Henry Lincoln, *The Holy Blood and the Holy Grail* (London, 1982, 2005 illustrated reprint).
20 Alan Grant, Frank Quitely et al., *Batman: The Scottish Connection* (London, 1998), pp. 30–31.
21 Ibid, pp. 28–29.
22 Dan Brown, *The Da Vinci Code* (London, 2003, 2004 reprint), from Chapter 104 onwards.
23 Ibid, p. 564.
24 Earl and Countess of Rosslyn, *Rosslyn Chapel*, p. 67.
25 Some purport that maize is depicted in the church (it is not), and use this as evidence for a Sinclair-led pre-Columbian 'discovery' of North America. This legend pushes back in time the history of whiteness on the continent, and is predictably popular among ethno-nationalists. The story is included on Rosslyn Chapel's official website, Rosslyn Chapel, 'Explore the Carvings', https://www.rosslynchapel.com/visit/things-to-do/explore-the-carvings/ [accessed 15 June 2021].
26 A number of scholars are undertaking important work on this topic. Most notably, this chapter is indebted to Drs Mary Rambaran-Olm and Rory MacLellan, the editor of this volume. Rambaran-Olm tweets under the handle @ISASaxonists and her public history is available on Medium.com and elsewhere, https://mrambaranolm.medium.com [accessed 15 June 2021]. See particularly https://twitter.com/ISASaxonists/status/1186306775328460800?s=20 for a list of essential resources [accessed June 15 2021]. For MacLellan, see 'Far-right Appropriations of the Medieval Military Orders', *The Mediæval Journal*, vol. 91 (2019), pp. 175–198.
27 Real medieval Templar flags were simply half black and half white, but this popular image of them persists.
28 For Breivik's manifesto see Andrew Elliott, *Medievalism, Politics and Mass Media: Appropriating the Middle Ages in the Twenty-First Century* (Cambridge, 2017), Chapter 6.
29 Elliott, *Medievalism*, see especially p. 170 for the easy spread of medieval memes.
30 David Wollenberg, 'The New Knighthood: Terrorism and the Medieval', *Postmedieval: A Journal of Medieval Cultural Studies*, vol. 5 (2014), p. 24.
31 MacLellan, 'Far-right Appropriations', p. 183.
32 Tim Wallace Murphy interviewed by Tracy Latz and Marion Ross: 'Rosslyn Chapel: Tim Wallace Murphy Shares His Thoughts', 'Shift Your Life TV', 9 May 2011, https://youtu.be/G72M2a48obc [accessed 15 June 2021].
33 Brown, *Da Vinci Code*, p. 348.
34 Ibid, p. 567 (original italics).
35 This is the tagline of *The Da Vinci Code* film trailer, dir. Ron Howard (Columbia Pictures, 2006).
36 Andrew Sinclair, *The Sword and the Grail* (London, 1993, 1994 reprint).
37 Ibid, p. 1.
38 Ibid, p. 2.
39 Robert Lomas, 'The Origins of Freemasonry', http://www.robertlomas.com/Freemason/Origins.html [accessed 15 June 2021].
40 Andrew Sinclair, *Rosslyn* (Edinburgh, 2005), p. 105.

41 Robert Ferguson, *Knights Templar and Scotland* (Stroud, 2010), cover and discussion pp. 123–24, 126.

42 The earliest description of the church (and pre-the nineteenth-century restorations) describes it as an image of St George. Robert Forbes, *An Account of the Chapel of Roslin by Philo Roskelynsis* (Edinburgh, 1774), p. 27.

43 See Steven Boardman, 'The Cult of Saint George in Scotland', in eds. Stephen Boardman, John Reuben Davies, and Eila Williamson, *Saints' Cults in the Celtic World* (Woodbridge, 2009), pp. 146–59.

44 Alan Butler and John Ritchie, *Rosslyn Chapel Decoded* (London, 2013), illustration 19.

45 P.L. Snow, *A Rosslyn Treasury: Stories and Legends from Rosslyn Chapel* (Edinburgh, 2009, 2017 reprint). p. 171.

46 Tim Wallace Murphy and Marilyn Hopkins, *Rosslyn: Guardian of the Secrets of the Holy Grail* (London, 1999); Dan Burstein (ed.), *Secrets of the Code: The Unauthorised Guide to the Mysteries Behind The Da Vinci Code* (London, 2004).

47 'Rosslyn Chapel: Scotland's Repository of the Key to the Holy Grail Code of Lucifer', https://www.angelfire.com/x-cain/rosslyn.html [accessed 15 June 2021].

48 Post to a discussion group on Stormfront (username: 'wessexandwhite', posted 15 January 2019). *David* Livingstone, *Terrorism and the Illuminati: A Three Thousand Year History* (self-published via Amazon.com, 2007), pp. 86–88, 265.

49 For a full exploration of KTI's use of Templar imagery see MacLellan: 'Far-right Appropriations'.

50 The Knights Templar Order International, 'FAQ', https://www.knightstemplarorder.com/faq, Companies House, record for 'Rosslyn Portal', https://find-and-update.company-information.service.gov.uk/company/NI647575, Rosslyn Portal (KTI shop webpage) https://rosslynportal.com/ [all accessed 15 June 2021].

51 KTI, 'Full Knight Package', https://www.knightstemplarorder.com/full-knight [accessed 15 June 2021].

52 KTI, 'Affiliate Membership Package', https://www.knightstemplarorder.com/affiliate_membership [accessed 15 June 2021].

53 For example, a 2017 edition of Ben Novak's podcast *Budapest Beacon* interviews journalist Péter Erdélyi and carefully details KTI's role in funding far-right Islamophobic and anti-immigrant proto militias in Hungary, https://soundcloud.com/budapest-beacon/nick-griffin-and-jim-dowson-expelled-from-hungary [accessed 15 June 2021].

54 Simon Cox and Anna Meisel, 'Is this Britain's Most Influential Far-Right Activist?', BBC News (1 May 2019), https://www.bbc.co.uk/news/uk-43924702 [accessed 15 June 2021].

55 Dowson's Twitter account has since been suspended.

56 The KTI's FAQ has a section specifically about Freemasonry, which they deny all links to and accuse of being 'corrupt' and promoting the 'liberal subversion of Christian society', https://www.knightstemplarorder.com/faq [accessed 15 June 2021].

Bibliography

Primary Sources

Calendar of Scottish Supplications to Rome: vol.vi, 1471–92. eds. Alan Macquarrie, Roland Tanner, and Annie Dunlop. Edinburgh: Scottish Records Society, 2017.

Companies House record of 'Rosslyn Portal'. https://find-and-update.companyinformation.service.gov.uk/company/NI647575 [accessed 15 June 2021].

Edinburgh, National Records of Scotland. GD18/5010.

Forbes, Robert. *An Account of the Chapel of Roslin by Philo Roskelynsis.* Edinburgh: William Auld, 1774.

The Records of the Synod of Lothian and Tweeddale 1589–96, 1640–49. ed. James Kirk. Edinburgh: Stair Society, 1977.

Secondary Sources

Baigent, Michael and Richard Leigh. *The Temple and the Lodge.* London: Corgi, 1988 (1990 reprint).

Baigent, Michael, Richard Leigh and Henry Lincoln. *The Holy Blood and the Holy Grail.* London: Jonathan Cape, 1982 (London: Random House, 2005 illustrated reprint).

Boardman, Stephen, John Reuben Davies and Eila Williamson (eds.). *Saints' Cults in the Celtic World.* Woodbridge: Boydell, 2009.

Brown, Dan. *The Da Vinci Code.* New York: Doubleday and Bantam Books, London: Transworld, 2003 (London: Corgi, 2004 reprint).

Burstein, Dan (ed.). *Secrets of the Code: The Unauthorised Guide to the Mysteries behind the Da Vinci Code.* London: Weidenfeld and Nicolson, 2004.

Butler, Alan and John Ritchie. *Rosslyn Chapel Decoded.* London: Watkins, 2013.

Cox, Simon and Anna Meisel. 'Is this Britain's Most Influential Far-right Activist?'. *BBC News* (1 May 2019), www.bbc.co.uk/news/uk-43924702 [accessed 15 June 2021].

Elliott, Andrew B. R. *Medievalism, Politics and Mass Media: Appropriating the Middle Ages in the Twenty-First Century.* Woodbridge: Boydell, 2017.

Ferguson, Robert. *The Knights Templar and Scotland.* Stroud: The History Press, 2010.

Grant, Alan, Frank Quitely, et al. *Batman: The Scottish Connection.* DC Comics, London: Titan Books, 1998.

Higgitt, John (ed.). *Medieval Art and Architecture in the Diocese of St Andrews.* Leeds: British Archaeological Association Conference Transactions, 14, 1994, pp. 99–107.

Howard, Ron, dir. *The Da Vinci Code* film trailer. Columbia Pictures, 2006.

Knights Templar Order International. www.knightstemplarorder.com, and their shop webpage 'Rosslyn Portal'. https://rosslynportal.com [both accessed 15 June 2021].

Latz, Tracy and Marion Ross. 'Rosslyn Chapel: Tim Wallace Murphy Shares His Thoughts'. 'Shift Your Life TV', 9 May 2011. https://youtu.be/G72M2a-48obc [accessed 15 June 2021].

Livingstone, David. *Terrorism and the Illuminati: A Three-Thousand Year History*. Charleston: BookSurge LLC, an Amazon.com company, 2007.

Lomas, Robert. 'The Origins of Freemasonry'. www.robertlomas.com/Freemason/Origins.html [accessed 15 June 2021].

MacLellan, Rory. 'Far-right Appropriations of the Medieval Military Orders'. *The Mediæval Journal*, 91:1 (2019), pp. 175–98.

Menzies, John. *Menzies' Scottish Tourist's Pocket Guide*. Edinburgh: John Menzies, 1852.

Novak, Ben. *Budapest Beacon*. https://soundcloud.com/budapest-beacon/nick-griffin-and-jim-dowson-expelled-from-hungary, 2017 [accessed 15 June 2021].

Partner, Peter. *The Murdered Magicians: The Templars and their Myth*. Oxford: Oxford University Press, 1982.

Rambaran-Olm, Mary (@ISASaxonists). https://twitter.com/ISASaxonists/status/1186306775328460800?s=20 [accessed 15 June 2021].

Rosslyn Chapel. 'Explore the Carvings'. www.rosslynchapel.com/visit/things-to-do/explore-the-carvings/ [accessed 15 June 2021].

'Rosslyn Chapel: Scotland's Repository of the Key to the Holy Grail Code of Lucifer'. www.angelfire.com/x-cain/rosslyn.html [accessed 15 June 2021].

Rosslyn, Helen and Angelo Maggi (eds.). *Rosslyn Chapel: Country of Painter and Poet*. Edinburgh: National Galleries of Scotland, 2002.

Sinclair, Andrew. *The Sword and the Grail*. London: Random House, 1993 (London: Arrow, 1994 reprint).

———. *Rosslyn*. Edinburgh: Birlinn, 2005.

Snow, P.L. *A Rosslyn Treasury: Stories and Legends from Rosslyn Chapel*. Edinburgh: Floris Books, 2009 (2017 reprint).

Stevenson, David. *The Origins of Freemasonry: Scotland's Century 1590–1710*. Cambridge: Cambridge University Press, 1988.

Swarbrick, Lizzie. 'The Medieval Art and Architecture of Scottish Collegiate Churches'. Unpublished PhD thesis, University of St Andrews, 2017.

The Earl and Countess of Rosslyn (St-Clair Erskine, Peter, and Rosslyn, Helen). *Rosslyn Chapel*. London: Scala, 2017.

Wallace Murphy, Tim and Marilyn Hopkins. *Rosslyn: Guardian of the Secrets of the Holy Grail*. London: Element, 1999.

Wilson, Christopher and Collin McWilliam. *Buildings of Scotland: Lothian Except Edinburgh*. Harmondsworth: Penguin, 1978.

Wollenberg, David. 'The New Knighthood: Terrorism and the Medieval'. *Postmedieval: A Journal of Medieval Cultural Studies*, 5 (2014), pp. 21–33.

3 Acquiring Heritage

The Venerable Order of St John and the Accumulation of Its Past (1858–1931)

Nigel Hankin

On 24th June 1893, the feast day of St John the Baptist, the Prince of Wales, in his role as Grand Prior, officially opened the newly restored St John's Gate, Clerkenwell as the headquarters of the Grand Priory of England of the Venerable Order of the Hospital of St John of Jerusalem (OSJ).[1] In the previous three decades the order had been transformed from a rather purposeless group of antiquarians and eccentrics into an important philanthropic organisation with royal approval. St John's Gate had been part of the Priory of England, centre of the English *'langue'*, or branch, of the Knights Hospitaller, a physical reminder of the order's medieval antecedents, so its re-occupation was of considerable symbolic significance.

However, the order's claim to descent from the medieval Knights Hospitaller was not undisputed. Reporting on the event, the *Morning Post* observed that, 'as it exists at present, the order is both a continuation and a revival of the old Hospitaller Order of St John of Jerusalem'.[2] This ambiguity was something the order was very sensitive about. Only a few weeks before the celebrations at St John's Gate, a letter to *The Times* stated that 'there is a charitable society in England which tries to pass itself off as a branch of the order' but that 'the claims of this society are based on garbled documents and on statements that are directly contrary to fact'.[3] Since the 1870s, the order had created the St John Ambulance Association, trained thousands in first aid at a time when industrial accidents were rife, and established the beginnings of an ambulance service where none had previously existed. In recognition of this it had received a royal charter in 1888. Yet despite this public validation of their activities the members of the OSJ still seem to have felt uneasy at any suggestion that their claims to medieval ancestry were bogus. As this chapter shall show, their collecting activities in this period can be seen partly as a reflection of this concern, reinforcing their collective self-image by acquiring pieces of

DOI: 10.4324/9781003200802-4

the order's heritage, and giving additional credibility to their philanthropic efforts.

The Order of St John in the Late Nineteenth Century

In 1798 Napoleon expelled the Hospitallers from Malta and they spent the next several decades in disarray. The French *langues*, restored in 1814, hoped to take advantage of the Greek struggle for independence to re-establish the order in the Mediterranean. Imagining that it would make it easier to get political support and money in London to sponsor such a venture, a handful of French knights explored the possibility of reviving the English *langue*, and in 1831 the Revd Robert Peat was elected prior of a restored English priory.[4] Peat and his associates contended that they were a continuation of the English order resurrected under Queen Mary in 1557 since, although Elizabeth I had seized their property, the organisation had never subsequently been dissolved. Over the following decades attempts to obtain official recognition from the revitalised Sovereign Military Order of Malta in Rome failed.[5] It proved impossible to reach a compromise whereby the legitimacy of the Protestant knights in England could be recognised by Rome without them acknowledging Papal authority.[6]

A final attempt in 1858 came to nothing. As Sir Edmund Lechmere was later to record, 'the Roman Knights suddenly attempted to cast off the acts of their predecessors and entered what has been called a "protest". [Since then] the English branch has been the object of jealousy and continuous attack'.[7] The following year it was reported that

> Grave doubts exist as to the legitimacy of this revived branch of the English *langue*. The authorities in supreme governance over the order at Rome deny its validity, and refuse to recognise it as an integral branch of the venerable order of St John.[8]

The Knights felt that their integrity was being questioned. At a time when it was not clear that the OSJ had either a mission or a future, these attacks were felt especially keenly.

With few members and little money, the OSJ in England in 1858 was, as it was later described, 'feeble and purposeless'.[9] Their main charitable efforts were directed at providing a healthy diet to the convalescent poor after their discharge from Charing Cross and King's College Hospitals. In 1872, the Revd John Woodward, one of the chaplains of the order, despaired at 'the degradation of so time-honoured an institution to the level of a mere charitable society for the distribution of soup'.[10] It was only in the late nineteenth century that the OSJ found a purpose. Members of the order had been the driving force behind the establishment of the National Aid Society to provide help to victims of the Franco-Prussian War of 1870–71, and it was that experience which convinced John Furley that mobilising aid once war had broken out was insufficient.[11] He felt there was a role to be played by the order in providing first aid training during peacetime so that trained medical help was available in the event of war. Furley, Lechmere, and Col Francis Duncan toured the country addressing meetings and encouraging the establishment of ambulance associations to provide instruction in first aid in what became known as the 'Ambulance Crusades'.

Subsequently, the trained volunteers were formed into ambulance brigades with equipment (often designed by Furley) to assist the injured and get them to hospital. By 1887 over 100,000 had received first aid training from the Association, and by 1905 there were 479 divisions of the Ambulance Brigade in England and Wales with 13,922 members.[12] Especially in the early years much was made of the usefulness of such training in wartime, but it was rapidly clear that there was also a huge need in a peacetime world fraught with danger, 'the war which went on from day to day in their streets, factories, and workshops'.[13] As Col R.J. Blackham wrote in his history of the order, published in 1921, 'the White Banner of St John [...] has waved over many a battlefield from Palestine in the eleventh century, to Flanders in the twentieth, and yet has achieved its greatest victories in time of peace'.[14]

At the same time that the order was pursuing this major charitable endeavour the members were also accumulating artefacts associated with their adopted ancestors. In a history of the collection, published in 1945, its first curator, Henry Fincham, recorded that by 1875 there was a library of 228 books, and a catalogue compiled in 1895 listed 438 items. By 1912 this had swollen to nearly 1800 books, paintings, and other objects.[15] Mostly these were donated by members, although funds were made available for purchases from 1901 and increased substantially in 1912, and in 1923 a separate museum room was created to display the acquired heritage that identified the order with its crusader past. The expansion of the collection went hand in hand with the expansion of the order's charitable activities, each validating the other. In 1888, reflecting on the previous few decades, Dr John Oakley, Dean of Manchester and a chaplain of the order, described how 'a few grave and public-spirited men have tried to keep alive an ancient and venerable society, with a definite purpose of benevolence to the sick and wounded in war, and of other forms of succour to suffering humanity'.[16] Collecting books, objects, and even buildings associated with the history of the Hospitallers helped reassure the members of the legitimacy of their claim to be 'an ancient and venerable society', constructing a synthetic memory in material form of an imagined collective past.

Romantic Medievalism and St John's Gate

From at least the 1160s St John's Gate, Clerkenwell had formed the entrance to the inner courtyard of the Priory of England.[17] It was substantially rebuilt by Prior Thomas Docwra (1501–27) and completed in 1504. It had been denuded of its battlements sometime in the 1760s as they had become unsafe, and by the 1850s it had become a pub called the Old Jerusalem Tavern decorated with suits of armour like the 'vault of some feudal ruin', and selling its own 'Chivalrie' gin.[18] (Figure 3.1) During the 1830s, the uncertain status of the fledgling OSJ had produced a rival organisation called the Knights of St John, and for a time they operated a dispensary for the sick poor and foreigners

ST. JOHN'S GATE, CLERKENWELL.

Figure 3.1 Unknown artist, St John's Gate, Clerkenwell. A view from the south side before the mid-century restoration. Nineteenth-century engraving. Ink on paper. Private Collection. Courtesy of Bridgeman Images.

from the ground floor of the west tower.[19] This desire to validate their humanitarian efforts by the physical association with what remained of the Hospitaller past continued with the OSJ. When the freehold of the Gate became available in 1873, Lechmere acquired it and leased part of the building to the order. By one account, Fincham claimed Lechmere had outbid Cardinal Wiseman, who wanted to acquire the building for the SMOM.[20] This seems unlikely as Wiseman had died in 1865, but the story reinforces the idea that acquiring the Gate was part of a rivalry for legitimacy. The physical re-occupation of the Hospitaller past was a concrete claim to that legitimacy.

The order acquired the freehold from Lechmere in 1887 and soon commissioned a much more significant redevelopment from John Oldrid Scott, son of the architect of the Victorian Gothic revival, Sir George Gilbert Scott. He employed a generic and rather heavy 'Tudor Gothic' to convey an appropriate sense of ancient military heritage (Figure 3.2). The reinstatement of the crenellations is typical of Victorian Gothic, re-imagining what is essentially a set of offices as a

Figure 3.2 St John's Gate, Clerkenwell. Illustration for *The Queen's London* (London: Cassell, 1896). This photo shows Oldrid Scott's restoration of the crenellations but predates the creation of the Chapter Hall in the space to the right. Private Collection. Courtesy of Bridgeman Images.

crusader castle. The panelling and armorial glass that were installed are also typical of neo-Gothic design, recreating an imagined medieval past as an appropriate setting for the self-proclaimed descendants of the Knights Hospitaller and as a home for their collection of objects associated with that history.

A further expansion of the building by Oldrid Scott in 1901–3 included the creation of the Chapter Hall, a large ceremonial space with a lantern ceiling and Perpendicular-style windows. The decoration of this important room can be seen as a physical assertion of the legitimacy of the English *langue* and its place within the wider order, emphasised by the arms of the different *langues* decorating the corbels supporting the roof beams. In the 1920s the arms of all the Priors of England, medieval and modern, were added to the panelling. In a bold statement of continuity, the centuries after Mary I are filled with the arms of holders of the office, albeit that they were based in Malta, before continuing with the arms of the Revd Peat in 1831.

The order also became more closely linked with the nearby parish church of St John, parts of which dated back to the medieval church of the priory. Lechmere acquired the advowson, which was transferred to the order in 1909, and the annual St John's Day service was held there from 1895.[21] From 1889, Oldrid Scott was involved in restoration work, partly funded by the order, including turning the middle aisle of the crypt, which dates back to the earliest days of the priory in the twelfth century, into a chapel.[22] The stained glass there today reuses glass originally installed in 1914 in the east window of the main church. It includes figures associated with the OSJ and the heraldry of the order and some of its English priors and knights (Figure 3.3). Once again, the order is re-occupying spaces associated with its supposed medieval predecessors and the decorative scheme asserts a link with that Hospitaller past.

The OSJ attracted men with antiquarian interests like Lechmere and Fincham, whose imagined Middle Ages was a romantic one of chivalrous knights and tournaments straight out of the pages of Sir Walter Scott. For them acquiring relics of the order's past served to reinforce their self-image as the heirs of the medieval Hospitallers, and nothing could be more iconic than St John's Gate. Writing in 1874, Lechmere felt that 'the interest which attaches to this relic of the ancient possessions of our order would amply compensate its members for any inconvenience'.[23] The Gate was used for meetings of the order's council from March 1874 and became a centre for the storage and distribution of first aid supplies and equipment for the St John Ambulance.[24] As Blackham later wrote, 'The glorious spirit of the old Knights must

Figure 3.3 The East Window of the Crypt of St John's, Clerkenwell, depicting Raymond du Puy (Hospitaller grandmaster, 1118–60), St John the Baptist, and St Ubaldesca (a sister of the order, canonised for charitable deeds and miracles). The glass, by Archibald K. Nicholson, dates from 1914 and was originally installed in the east window of the church. Courtesy of The Museum of the Order of St John (photograph © Peter Dazeley from his book *London Explored*).

inspire the Council located once more under the ancient roof-tree of the order'.[25] Even if Clerkenwell was now a poor neighbourhood full of noisome industries and crowded tenements, the Gate could serve as a simulacrum of a fortress from which the Knights could sally forth to do good deeds.[26]

Emulating the Crusaders: Bearers of the Cross

Whilst travelling in Italy in 1894, Lechmere acquired a processional cross decorated with the eight-pointed cross of the order (Figure 3.4). Made of silver plates on an oak core, attached to the front is an earlier figure of Christ crucified. Beneath this is a shield depicting a lion rampant which has been identified as the arms of Pierre Decluys, Grand Prior of France (1522–35), and on the reverse is a plate engraved 'F.P. DECLUYS 1527'. However, Fincham identified the arms as those of

Figure 3.4 Processional Cross, 1527, silver on oak, with an earlier figure.
French. 46 × 55 cm. Museum of the Order of St John, London.
LDOSJ 659. Courtesy of the Museum of the Order of St John.

Prior Robert Mallory (1433–40). In December 1904, in a letter to Col
Sir Herbert Perrott, secretary of the order, he wrote that the shield:

> bears the arms of Mallory, Grand Prior of Clerkenwell and [...] my
> theory is that it was made for Mallory and belonged to our priory.
> The cross is early Italian Renaissance work but the shield of arms
> is quite Gothic in character and may have been affixed after it
> came to England.[27]

He also suggested that the cross should be carried in procession on
St John's Day, as it still is.[28] Fincham's keenness to connect the cross
with the English *langue* is particularly interesting. Overlooking the evidence of the engraved plaque he found reason to associate it with the
knights of Clerkenwell. In his desire to underscore the English order's

validity he is happy to romanticise a connection with its distant past that was entirely spurious.

Lechmere may have been being disingenuous when he claimed 'this Order of St John was simply a revived English branch of the old Order of Malta' but it was to the supposed piety and charity of the medieval Hospitallers that he referred when he stated that the order's 'usefulness and philanthropic nature were based on historic chivalry'.[29] Motives of Christian idealism and piety were ascribed to the crusader knights, and it was this benevolent aspect of the Hospitaller past that the order was keen to co-opt to validate their philanthropy. As well as the processional cross, other religious artefacts were acquired, including two chasubles purchased in 1913 embroidered with the arms of Grandmasters Perellos (1697–1720) and Cotoner (1663–80), and a silver chalice given by Vere, Lady Galway in 1910, allegedly brought to England by Philip II on his marriage to Mary I. As the *Pall Mall Gazette* observed in 1893, 'Any one fortunate to visit St John's Gate and meet the industrious secretary, Mr Easterbrook, in his comfortable office, finds him surrounded by relics of the former days of the order, as well as signs of its present activity'.[30] The quasi-religious overtones of the term 'relic' suggest that the collection of historic objects somehow sanctified their 'present activity'.

From the mid-nineteenth century the Anglican Church was also trying to counter the perceived 'feminisation' of religion, with churchgoing increasingly seen as the province of women.[31] Churchmen and writers such as Charles Kingsley and Thomas Hughes looked for examples of Christian heroism that showed religious belief was compatible with masculinity.[32] Crusader knights provided the perfect example of this 'muscular Christianity'.[33] Earlier in the century Kenelm Digby had depicted the Crusades as combining chivalric and Christian values in a way that a Victorian gentleman should emulate.[34] That for much of their history the Hospitallers had been a maritime organisation countering piracy in the Mediterranean was largely ignored in how the order portrayed itself. Although views of Malta and scenes of naval engagements with corsairs also formed part of the collection in this period, it was the military and medical elements of the Hospitaller past that were promoted, for example in the Ambulance Crusades. The religious zealotry of the crusader knights was also overlooked. In 1879 *Jackson's Oxford Journal* described how:

> The Knights of St John of Jerusalem, who had inaugurated this movement, were [...] one of the most chivalrous, and noble, [...] of the great guilds or associations of the Middle Ages, and the objects

of love, charity, and chivalry which first founded them [were] everlasting principles. It was a Society which based itself on a long line of charity, love and good works, and it was showing how some of these old principles might be applied to modern civilisation.[35]

As the *Western Daily Press* remarked in 1901, 'The spirit of valour, mercy, and self-sacrifice which the Knights Hospitaller were in the romantic middle ages the incarnation, still lives vigorously in our prosaic modern world'.[36] Invoking their imagined crusader past to inspire their volunteers and raise funds was true from the very beginnings of the St John Ambulance, but was especially the case in times of war. In 1914 an illustration that appeared in *Punch* portrays this idea of the work of the St John Ambulance amongst the troops being blessed by the spirit of their crusader past (Figure 3.5). For an organisation about to provide valuable assistance to the war effort, it was to the muscular Christianity of their supposed medieval antecedents that they looked for inspiration.

This genuflecting to a largely bogus past whilst creating an organisation to deal with the very real needs of the modern world is a

Figure 3.5 Poster produced by Jordan Gaskell Ltd, London, 1914. Ink on Paper. 160 × 110 cm. Museum of the Order of St John, London. LDOSJ 9118. Courtesy of the Museum of the Order of St John.

leitmotif of the OSJ in this period. In acquiring artefacts associated with the Hospitallers they seem to be wishing to sanctify their current activities, their re-imagined crusading past providing assurance that their philanthropic work was both proper and manly. Ignoring the order's maritime heritage and focusing instead on its medical activities in the Holy Land they used selected aspects of their supposed past to promote involvement in the St John Ambulance as noble, Christian work. As Blackham asserted, 'the St John Ambulance had its roots in the earliest years of chivalry when the Knights of St John combined [...] the art of healing with valour and prowess as soldiers'.[37] In emulating their re-interpreted version of their Hospitaller antecedents they were manufacturing a collective self-image that emphasised the pious heroism of the knights of old. The cross that Lechmere acquired may have had nothing to do with the medieval English *langue*, but it was a tangible reminder that they, like their forbears, were doing God's work.

The Order of St John and Empire: Cannonballs and Ophthalmology

From its earliest days the order seems to have had an eye to British imperial interests in the Mediterranean where there was an obvious overlap with their Hospitaller past. The revival of the order in England had its origins in thoughts of military adventure as the Ottoman Empire began to crumble, and in 1841 one member, Sir William Hillary, had written a pamphlet advocating a new crusade.[38] By the 1850s all dreams of military glory had been abandoned. Nonetheless, reconnecting with their crusader past did not stop at St John's Gate. Members of the order added physical reminders of the OSJ's history in the Mediterranean to the collection throughout the period. In 1902 Lady Lechmere donated an early sixteenth-century breastplate that had allegedly been used by the Knights on Rhodes, complete with bullet hole. Furley acquired some stone cannonballs from Malta, and Lady Strangford donated two iron cannonballs from Rhodes.[39] On a larger scale, in 1911 the order began negotiations to acquire the fifteenth-century Hospitaller castle at Kolossi in Cyprus and, in the early 1920s, part of the English 'Auberge' in Rhodes – which had been the hostel for the English knights there – was acquired by Sir Vivian Gabriel, a Knight of Justice, and subsequently bequeathed to the order.[40]

Moreover, the desire to re-establish the order in Jerusalem did not stop with Hillary. As early as 1873, Lechmere, in his role as secretary, recorded in the annual report that:

[a] subject which has from time to time occupied the attention of the Chapter for some years [...] has lately been more prominently brought before our notice, which is the possible acquisition of a site within the walls of Jerusalem, the cradle of our Order, with a view to the ultimate establishment of some such Hospitaller object as a British hospice [and] to secure, if possible, part of the ancient Hospital of St John.[41]

Unfortunately, the Prussian order of St John acquired most of the site before the English could act and attempts to acquire the remaining section came to nothing.[42] As with St John's Gate, the acquisition and physical re-occupation of the Hospitaller past is a reflection of the OSJ's preoccupation with their heritage as the heart of their self-image and collective identity, re-occupying the sites of their past as validation of their activities in the present. The direct echoing of the order's medieval medical heritage in Jerusalem is obvious and the re-establishment of the order's links with the Holy Land was explicit in their appeal for funds:

Those who belong to the English branch of the order of St John are justified in looking for liberal assistance towards the expense of maintaining the hospice. The great nations of the Continent have their hospitals at Jerusalem; and this country [...] will surely be willing to sustain an undertaking which [...] claims the support of hospitallers as connected with the earliest home of the order and of Christians as a work of humanity, established in the birthplace of their Faith.[43]

It was also part of a wider British imperial mission to preserve ancient sites in a way that the local inhabitants were deemed incapable of doing. As Swenson has argued, 'Across Europe the protection of monuments explicitly became a symbol of a nation's ability to rule overseas – a measure of civilisation', justifying paternalistic and imperialistic assertions of stewardship over other territories. The British, as well as vying for political advantage in the tottering Ottoman Empire, were implicitly pursuing what they saw as their imperial mission to bring civilisation to local populations regarded as incapable of fending for themselves.[44] Or, as the *Pall Mall Gazette* reported in 1893, the order 'support[s] an ophthalmic hospital at Jerusalem, where it is much needed, since the modern Canaanite is much too lazy to wash out of his eyes the dust and insects that gather in them'.[45]

The OSJ's engagement with the Near East fits into the Victorian re-imagining of the crusades as a 'civilising' mission amongst 'backwards' peoples, bringing medical aid to the locals and reinforcing British 'soft' power whilst asserting their legitimacy by re-occupying sites associated with the order's past. The idea of returning to 'the cradle of our Order' had long been entertained in England, almost as an obligation imposed by their past. In the event it went hand in hand with competition amongst the European powers to gain influence in the crumbling Ottoman Empire, justifying their involvement by providing medical services to the local people and preserving selected aspects of their heritage. Further afield, the exporting of the St John Ambulance became part of the network of empire, and by 1905 there were 50 brigade divisions overseas, in New Zealand, Australia, South Africa, and India.[46] As King later wrote, the St John Ambulance had 'become one of the firmest links in that sacred chain of loyalty which binds together the Dominions and Colonies in affectionate and devoted service to their King-Emperor'.[47] Even as they were acquiring the armour and armaments of the order's bloody military past they were also engaged in a 'civilising' and life-saving mission across the British Empire and beyond.

Collecting and Collective Identity

By the time of the centenary of its revival in 1931, the order had become so much more than what Oakley described as an 'ancient and honourable guild of good breeding and good works'.[48] Yet in their collecting activities and in the promotion of their work they were continually gesturing to that ancient past, and this sense of historic continuity was a key part of how they saw themselves and wanted to be perceived. Their collection served to promote what Cubitt has described as 'concepts of collective identity or corporate continuity that foster the fiction of collective memory'.[49] In acquiring the physical remains of the order in Clerkenwell they were literally occupying the Hospitallers' heritage, using it both as a centre for the St John Ambulance and as a home for their collection of books and artefacts associated with the order's history, asserting their claim to that history by acquiring pieces of it. Sanctifying their actions by collecting 'relics' gave them legitimacy and status in the eyes of their own members, as well as external recognition. As Misztal has argued, it is 'the presentation of the past, both that shared by a group and that which is collectively commemorated that enacts and gives substance to the group's identity, its present conditions and its vision of the future'.[50]

Their collecting activities encompassed the Hospitallers' heritage well beyond the English *langue*, co-opting their Mediterranean history as well. Even when the original items were not available the order

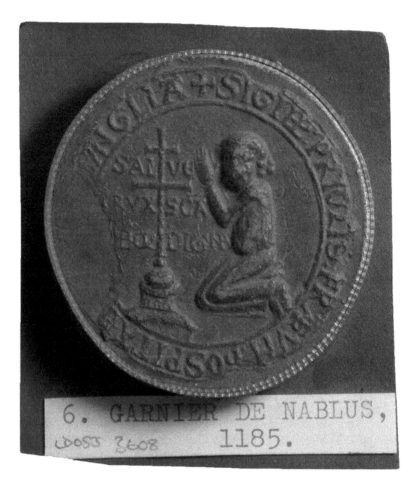

Figure 3.6 Cast of the seal of Garnier de Nablus, Prior of England and later
Grand Master of the Knights Hospitaller (d. 1192). The original
seal dates from 1185 and is in the British Library. Wax. 54 mm in
diameter. The Museum of the Order of St John, London. LDOSJ
3608. The replica was one of a number given in 1914 by W. Barclay Squire (Museum of the Order of St John and University of
Birmingham 2016).

was happy to make do with replicas – literally fabricating their history.
Copies of Hospitaller seals were donated by Barclay Squire in 1914
(Figure 3.6). On a larger scale the order acquired casts of crusader
tombs from the Musée Cluny in Paris in the mid-1920s. Reminders of

the past – genuine or replica – served to sustain the idea of a continuous existence, projecting backwards a current perception of identity that drew on particular elements of Victorian crusader myth-making. The attitude to the past also shifted as the members of the OSJ discovered a sense of purpose. In 1864 the chancellor of the OSJ, Sir John St George, disconsolately described the knights as 'very famous in the history of past times but comparatively unsuited to the present'.[51] By 1880, however, Lechmere was much more positive about the 'value of antiquity', and expressed confidence that the order 'was quite as well adapted to the nineteenth century as it was for the time when it was founded'.[52] Cementing ties with their medieval Hospitaller past helped foster that new-found sense of purpose. Their activities extended to acquiring and re-occupying sites of particular symbolic significance in their supposed crusader past, exemplifying what Nora describes as *lieux de mémoire*, places imbued with particular significance in the collective memory.[53] The acquisition of St John's Gate, the establishment of a hospital in Jerusalem, and the attempted purchase of the castle at Kolossi all exemplify the OSJ's active re-occupation of its symbolic material heritage. Buildings and objects became the material building blocks of a collective synthetic memory.

Conclusion

In the centenary celebrations in 1931 Lord Scarborough, the sub-prior, was careful to emphasise that 'the purpose was to celebrate a Revival, not a creation'.[54] The contested nature of its history made the OSJ peculiarly sensitive to the question of heritage. Lechmere and the other key figures in the OSJ deployed the crusader image to promote the work of the St John Ambulance, tapping into the Victorian re-imaging of the crusader knight as the image of heroism, morality, and masculinity. Cementing their ties to a long and distinguished history by acquiring books, objects, and buildings associated with the Hospitallers in their heyday, they reinforced that image and their own sense of collective identity, of validation and legitimacy, as well as creating a powerful promotional tool. Theirs was a fractured identity – looking to the past as both a justification and a responsibility, whilst also looking forward to the needs of a dangerous modern world. The OSJ's acquisition of St John's Gate, and the decorative schemes employed there and in the nearby church, the establishment of a hospital in Jerusalem and their accumulation of artefacts all asserted the continuity of the order's history and its links with a romanticised medieval past. They saw their charitable work as blessed by the spirit of their pious and heroic crusader predecessors, their supposed past serving as a source of inspiration for their charitable endeavours in the present. That history gave them both a sense of collective identity and a mission.

Notes

1 As it was styled in the royal charter of 1888. Hereafter referred to as the OSJ or the order.
2 *Morning Post*, 26 June 1893, p. 4.
3 *The Times*, 6 April 1893, p. 2.
4 Jonathan Riley-Smith, 'The Order of St John in England 1827–58', in *The Military Orders: Fighting for the Faith*, ed. Malcolm Barber (London: Variorum, 1994), pp. 121–38.
5 The Sovereign Military Hospitaller Order of St John of Jerusalem of Rhodes and Malta, usually abbreviated to the Sovereign Military Order of Malta or SMOM.
6 Helen Nicholson, *The Knights Hospitaller* (London: Boydell Press, 2013), p. 143.
7 London, The Museum of the Order of St John (MOSJ) T26.3. Letter from Lechmere to the editor of the *Morning Post*, 24 April 1873. Sir Edmund Lechmere, MP, was a philanthropist, antiquarian, and a leading figure in the OSJ in the late 19th century.
8 'Literary Review', *John Bull and Britannia*, 8 January 1859, p. 26.
9 E. Walford, *In Memoriam. Sir Edmund A. H. Lechmere, Baronet* (1895), p. 23.
10 MOSJ Late 19th Century Correspondence. Woodward to Gould-Weston, 23 February 1872.
11 The British National Society for Aid to the Sick and Wounded in War, or the National Aid Society was the precursor of the British Red Cross. Furley was also associated with the founding of the Red Cross movement.
12 Ronnie Cole-Mackintosh, *A Century of Service to Mankind: A History of the St John Ambulance Brigade* (London: Century Banham, 1986), p. 25; Nigel Corbet Fletcher, *The St John Ambulance Association, Its History, and Its Part in the Ambulance Movement* (London: St John Ambulance Association, 1929), p. 49.
13 'Aid to the Injured', *Leicester Chronicle and the Leicestershire Mercury*, 17 January 1880, p. 3.
14 Col R.J. Blackham, *The White Cross of St John* (Bombay: G.W. Claridge, 1921), p. 49.
15 Henry Fincham, *Notes on the History of the Library and the Museum of the Venerable Order of the Hospital of St John of Jerusalem* (London: private publication, 1945).
16 Dr John Oakley, 'The Order of St John', *Manchester Guardian*, 25 July 1888, p. 5.
17 Barney Sloane and Gordon Malcolm, *Excavations at the Priory of the Order of the Hospital of St John of Jerusalem, Clerkenwell, London* (London: Museum of London Archaeology Service, 2004), p. 39.
18 'St John's Gate and St John's Lane' in *Survey of London: Vol 46, South and East Clerkenwell*, ed. Philip Temple (London, 2008), pp. 142–63. British

History Online https://www.british-history.ac.uk/survey-london/vol46/pp142-163 [accessed 9 April 2019].

19 Ibid.

20 Sir Edwin King, *The Knights of St John in the British Realm*, revised by Sir Harry Luke (London: Hills and Lacy, 1967), p. 146.

21 'St John's Church and St John's Square' in *Survey of London: Vol 46, South and East Clerkenwell*, ed. Philip Temple (London, 2008), pp. 115–41. British History Online https://www.british-history.ac.uk/survey-london/vol46/pp115-141 [accessed 9 April 2019].

22 Ibid.

23 MOSJ, *Annual Report of the Order of St John 1874*, p. 11.

24 *Survey of London: Vol 46, South and East Clerkenwell*, pp. 142–63.

25 Blackham, *White Cross*, p. 29.

26 Charles Booth's survey in the summer of 1898 found the area rather squalid, noting a 'fearful stench' from a Gorgonzola factory. A tin-plater's works stood next to the gate for much of the 19th century (British Library of Political and Economic Science, Booth survey notebooks, B353, pp. 156–59).

27 MOSJ T26.3. Fincham to Perrott, 20 December 1904.

28 Or at least a copy of it is.

29 'Aid to the Injured', *Jackson's Oxford Journal*, 22 March 1879, p. 6.

30 'The Order of St John', *Pall Mall Gazette*, 24 June 1893, p. 3.

31 Adam Knobler, 'Holy Wars, Empires, and the Portability of the Past: The Modern Uses of Medieval Crusades', *Comparative Studies in Society and History* Vol. 48 (2006), pp. 293–325, 311.

32 Olive Anderson, 'The Growth of Christian Militarism in Mid-Victorian Britain', *The English Historical Review* Vol. 86, No. 338 (1971), pp. 46–72, 39.

33 Mike Horswell, *The Rise and Fall of British Crusader Medievalism, c. 1825–1945* (Abingdon: Routledge, 2018) pp. 39–44.

34 Mark Girouard, *Return to Camelot* (London: Yale University Press, 1981), p. 56. The first two editions of Digby's *Broad Stone of Honour* were subtitled *Rules for the Gentlemen of England*, whilst later editions bore the subtitle *The True Sense and Practice of Chivalry*.

35 'Aid to the Injured', *Jackson's Oxford Journal*, 22 March 1879, p. 6.

36 *Western Daily Press,* 13 February 1901, p. 7.

37 Blackham, *White Cross*, p. 49.

38 Elizabeth Siberry, *The New Crusaders* (Abingdon: Routledge, 2016), pp. 76–82. Appendix B reproduces the text of the pamphlet.

39 MOSJ *Annual Report,* June 1879, p. 10.

40 King, *Knights of St John in the British Realm*, pp. 218–20.

41 MOSJ *Annual Report,* June 1873, p. 11.

42 The Prussian Order, the *Johanniterorden*, was refounded in 1852 by Frederick William IV.

43 *Berrow's Worcester Journal*, 3 November 1883, p. 6.

44 Astrid Swenson, 'The Heritage of Empire', in *From Plunder to Preservation: Britain and the Heritage of Empire, c1800–1940*, eds. A. Swenson and P. Mandler, Proceedings of the British Academy 187 (Oxford, 2013), p. 10.

45 'The Order of St John', *Pall Mall Gazette*, 24 June 1893, p. 3.

46 Corbet Fletcher, pp. 49–50. By 1912 there were also divisions in Sri Lanka, Canada, and Malta.

47 King, *Knights of St John in the British Realm*, p. 148.

48 Dr John Oakley, 'The Order of St John', *Manchester Guardian*, 25 July 1888, p. 5.
49 Geoffrey Cubitt, *History and Memory* (Manchester: Manchester University Press, 2007), p. 19.
50 Barbara Misztal, *Theories of Social Remembering* (Maidenhead: Open University Press, 2003), p. 7.
51 MOSJ T26.3. St George to Bigsby, 12 January 1864.
52 'Aid to the Injured', *Leicester Chronicle and the Leicestershire Mercury*, 17 January 1880, p. 3.
53 Pierre Nora, 'From *Lieux de mémoire* to *Realms of Memory*', in *Realms of Memory*, ed. Pierre Nora, 3 vols (New York: Columbia University Press, 1996), I, p. xvi.
54 *The Centenary of the Revival of the Order of St John in England, 1931* (London: St John's Gate, Clerkenwell, 1932), p. v.

Bibliography

Unpublished Primary Sources

Archives of the Museum and Library of the Most Venerable Order of St John of Jerusalem, London.

Published Primary Sources

Books and Pamphlets

Blackham, R.J. *The White Cross of St John.* Bombay: G.W. Claridge, 1921.
Corbet Fletcher, Nigel. *The St John Ambulance Association, Its History, and Its Part in the Ambulance Movement.* London: St John Ambulance Association, 1929.
Fincham, H.W. *Notes on the History of the Library and the Museum of the Venerable Order of the Hospital of St John of Jerusalem.* London: private publication, 1945.
The Centenary of the Revival of the Order of St John in England, 1931. London: St John's Gate, Clerkenwell, 1932.
Walford, Edward. *In Memoriam Sir Edmund A.H. Lechmere, Baronet.* London: Cull & Son, 1895.

Newspapers

Berrow's Worcester Journal, 3 November 1883.
Jackson's Oxford Journal, 22 March 1879.
John Bull and Britannia, 8 January 1859.
The Leicester Chronicle and Leicestershire Mercury, 17 January 1880; 25 October 1890.

The Manchester Guardian, 25 July 1888.
The Morning Post, 26 June 1893.
The Pall Mall Gazette, 24 June 1893.
The Times, various.
The Western Daily Press, 13 February 1901.

Secondary Sources

Anderson, Olive. 'The Growth of Christian Militarism in Mid-Victorian Britain'. *The English Historical Review* Vol. 86, No. 338 (1971), pp. 46–72.

Cole-Mackintosh, Ronnie. *A Century of Service to Mankind: A History of the St John Ambulance Brigade*. London: Century Banham, 1986.

Cubitt, Geoffrey. *History and Memory*. Manchester: Manchester University Press, 2007.

Girouard, Mark. *Return to Camelot*. London: Yale University Press, 1981.

Horswell, Mike. *The Rise and Fall of British Crusader Medievalism, c. 1825–1945*. Abingdon: Routledge, 2018.

Hospitallers: The History of the Order of St John. London: Hambledon Press, 1999.

King, Sir Edwin. *The Knights of St John in the British Realm*. revised by Sir Harry Luke. London: Hills and Lacy, 1967.

Knobler, Adam. 'Holy Wars, Empires, and the Portability of the Past: The Modern Uses of Medieval Crusades'. *Comparative Studies in Society and History*, Vol. 48 (2006), pp. 293–325.

Misztal, Barbara. *Theories of Social Remembering*. Maidenhead: Open University Press, 2003.

Nicholson, Helen J. *The Knights Hospitaller*. London: Boydell Press, 2013.

Nora, Pierre. 'From *Lieux de mémoire* to *Realms of Memory*'. In *Realms of Memory*, ed. Pierre Nora, 3 vols. New York: Columbia University Press, 1996, pp. xv–xxiv.

Riley-Smith, Jonathan. 'The Order of St John in England 1827–58'. In *The Military Orders: Fighting for the Faith*, ed. Malcolm Barber. London: Variorum, 1994, pp. 121–38.

Siberry, Elizabeth. *The New Crusaders*. Abingdon: Routledge, 2016.

Sloane, Barney and Gordon Malcolm. *Excavations at the Priory of the Order of the Hospital of St John of Jerusalem, Clerkenwell, London*. London: Museum of London Archaeology Service, 2004.

Swenson, Astrid. 'The Heritage of Empire'. In *From Plunder to Preservation: Britain and the Heritage of Empire, c1800–1940*, eds. A. Swenson and P. Mandler, Proceedings of the British Academy 187. Oxford: Oxford University Press, 2013, pp. 3–28.

Online

Bearers of the Cross: Material Religion in the Crusading World, 1095-c.1300
https://www.bearersofthecross.org.uk/project/ [accessed 2 March 2019].

'St John's Church and St John's Square'. In *Survey of London: Vol 46, South and East Clerkenwell*, ed. Philip Temple. London, 2008, pp. 115–41. *British History Online* https://www.british-history.ac.uk/survey-london/vol46/pp115-141 [accessed 9 April 2019].

'St John's Gate and St John's Lane'. In *Survey of London: Vol 46, South and East Clerkenwell*, ed. Philip Temple. London, 2008, pp. 142–63. *British History Online* https://www.british-history.ac.uk/survey-london/vol46/pp142-163 [accessed 9 April 2019].

4 Reconstructing the Past

The Memory and Tradition of the Order of the Hospitaller Knights of Saint John in Modern Greece (Nineteenth and Twentieth Centuries)

Photeine V. Perra

This chapter shall provide an overview of how modern Greeks have perceived the memory of the Hospitallers and in what ways this has manifested, focusing on several aspects that indicate the way in which this memory of the order has been preserved. The first is in the academic study of the Hospitallers' history in Greece by Greek scholars studying the pertinent written sources. This exploration will also include the field of archaeology as well as the preservation of those monuments that are connected to the Hospitallers' history in the country. It will also examine a particularly important period in modern Rhodian and Dodecanesian history, that of the Italian occupation (1912–43), which repeatedly attempted to revive the splendour of Hospitaller rule. Another important element is the literary depiction of the order's presence by contemporary Greeks and in what ways this perception is expressed in various literary works. Finally, this chapter will examine whether the order is perceived positively or negatively in the collective consciousness of the Greek people and especially among Rhodians and other Dodecanesians.

Seven centuries have passed since the Order of the Hospitallers introduced a new chapter of late medieval history following its establishment in Greek lands and more specifically on the island of Rhodes and its Dodecanesian territory between 1306 and 1309/1310. The Knights Hospitaller of Saint John remained in the Aegean Sea until 1522/1523, that is, for over two centuries, with a continuous presence that left a deep historical footprint in all the territories under their rule.

There has been an extensive bibliography concerning the Hospitallers in Greece, enlightening many aspects of their history and presence in Helladic lands.[1] What has seen less study is the impact of their

DOI: 10.4324/9781003200802-5

occurrence and the perception of their rule in the collective subconscious of modern Greece. In this chapter we shall attempt to examine how the memory of the Hospitallers in modern Greece was preserved and how far it is viewed positively or negatively by Greeks today.

The Study of the Hospitallers in Greek Academia: A Brief Survey

In modern Greece, Hospitaller History is seen through the prism of a broader chapter of Greek history that began following the first capture of Constantinople in 1204 by the Fourth Crusade: namely, the 'Latinocracy' (*Λατινοκρατία*), the era in which Latin (i.e. Catholic Western European) rulers occupied Greek lands formerly belonging to the Byzantine Empire. A special chapter of this period concerns the two centuries of the Knights Hospitallers' rule on Rhodes and the other Dodecanesian islands, known as 'the Rule of the Knights', '*Ιπποτοκρατία*', and the subject of a rich and important bibliography by both Greek and other scholars.[2]

The systematic study of the Hospitaller's past in Greece commenced shortly before the mid-twentieth century. One of the first and most important Greek scholars to deal with the Knights was Ioannes Ch. Delendas (1890–1964?), an eminent scholar whose monograph on the Hospitallers was published in 1947 and was reissued in 1955. Delendas' origins were in the island of Santorini and more specifically from the noble house of Delenda, a Catalan family that settled in Greece during the Latinocracy.[3] His book *The Knights of Rhodes* was the first in Greek to deal with the Hospitaller's past including their history not only in Rhodes but also in Jerusalem and Malta.[4] His decision to write the book was dictated by the fact that he himself was a member of the Hospitaller Order. Delendas' book is still used in Greek historiography, despite the fact that the field has since progressed significantly.

The next important scholar is Christodoulos I. Papachristodoulou (1899–1988 or 1989), who wrote a classic of the historiography of the regional history of Greece.[5] This work consists of a detailed history of the Island of Rhodes, with important additions on that of its surrounding area, following the pattern established by several modern Greek authors who had often tackled the topic of regional history. Papachristodoulou succeeded in producing a well-researched and balanced account of the Rhodian past, paying particular attention to the period of the Hospitaller occupation, thus offering valuable material for furthering the study of this crucial period of the island's history.[6] His account of the Hospitallers was mainly based on the Hospitaller and historian Giacomo Bosio's (1544–1627) works, also translating into Greek a few extracts from Bosio's writings.[7]

Another important scholar who also successfully 'introduced' the Knights Hospitaller to a wider reading public was Elias Kollias (1936–2007), ephor (a senior official) of Byzantine Antiquities from 1966 to 1998, who did much to promote the Rhodian and Dodecanesian medieval past. His great contributions were not limited to his purely archaeological work, he also worked to disseminate the multi-faceted historical presence of the order through a variety of other aspects like its economic organization and its social life. Of particular importance was Kollias' work on the order's contacts and relations with their Greek subjects.[8] Elias Kollias' historiographical contribution will indubitably remain invaluable and fundamental for researchers of the history of the order in Greece and its islands.[9]

Yet another prominent Greek scholar who has contributed significantly to the study of the order's history and civilization in Greek lands is Professor Zacharias N. Tsirpanles, who has taught medieval history to generations of students in the Universities of Ioannina and Thessalonica. His contributions are of major importance, since his researches in the Hospitaller archives make him the first and most important Greek scholar who has dealt with the order's history through the publication of primary sources. His publications remain central for anyone attempting to undertake research on the order and its presence in the Dodecanese, since, in addition to his editions of primary source documents, he has investigated in depth several major issues relating to the Order's rule, both in his erudite synthetic works and in specialized studies and articles.[10]

A general comment regarding the attitude of these historians towards the history of the order would be that they definitely did not treat it with prejudice or enmity. As a common rule, they primarily based their conclusions on archival and scholarly testimony, while avoiding providing either a negative or positive slant in their narratives. They invariably present the period of the Hospitaller occupation as an integral part of the history of Rhodes and the Dodecanese.

Hospitaller Monuments in Greece and Archaeological Research

In addition to the activities on the part of researchers and the academic community, it is useful to consider a crucial parameter regarding the Order's presence, which reflects on today through the Hospital's monuments not only on Rhodes but also in the Dodecanesian area. These, in addition to the celebrated Palace of the Grand Master in Rhodes Town, include impressive fortifications, temples, churches and other installations which facilitated the various needs of the Hospitallers.

Following the Ottoman conquest by Suleiman II 'the Law-giver' (or 'the Magnificent') and the ensuing departure of the order from Rhodes, the island, together with the rest of the Twelve Islands ('on iki ada' in Turkish), remained under Ottoman domination from 1523 to 1912. In the course of the nineteenth century, still under Ottoman control, Rhodes was to become an object of interest on the part of various travellers, among which the case of the Swedish Johannes Hedenborg (1800–70) was the most interesting.[11] This widely travelled and talented physician and historian decided to spend the final phase of his life on the island, residing there for over 20 years from 1840 to 1864. He harboured a special interest and affection for Rhodes, if we are to judge by the five-volume work which he composed on the island's history. Hedenborg's testimony is of critical value, since he has preserved in his writings a particularly clear picture of Rhodes and its medieval monuments which, it seems, were left in a lamentable condition in the mid-nineteenth century. Nothing whatsoever reminded one of the former fame of the Knights of Saint John. Whatever monuments remained were in ruins. No interest whatsoever in the relics of the Hospitaller was displayed by the Ottoman authorities, with the result being their total abandonment to the inevitable ravages of time. In addition, and especially during the latter part of the nineteenth century, natural phenomena like earthquakes, as well as an explosion in the Hospitaller Palace's powder magazine, caused extensive devastation and damage to medieval Rhodes Town.[12]

This neglect was to change after 1912, with the arrival of the Italians, who seized control in the Dodecanese until 1943, when the area was eventually incorporated into the modern Greek state (the then-Kingdom of Greece).[13] In building construction the Italians adopted a policy characterized by Tsirpanles as the 'policy of the stone'. Among the various building projects the Italians restored many monuments associated with the Rhodian Hospitaller past, which they attempted to utilize as a means of propaganda in order to 'legitimize' their rights of possession over the Twelve Islands.[14] In this framework we can put the visit to Rhodes of the Grand Master of the Sovereign Military Order of Malta, Ludovico Chigi della Rovere Albani, which took place on September 1931. He was invited to participate in the ecclesiastical congress that had been organized for the 1,500-year anniversary of the Ephesus Synod of A.D. 431, which had condemned Nestorianism, and his presence was an attempt to underline the so-called 'connection' with the Hospitaller Order and the need of the Italian occupation to appear as the historical continuation of Hospitaller rule. This was indeed an event of crucial importance for local population's future views of the Hospitaller past in the area and imposed a negative atmosphere which lingered on in future years, creating a dark association in the eyes of the Greeks for the historical memory of the Hospitaller presence in Rhodes and the Twelve Islands.

Thus, in the aforementioned 'Italian' period excavations were undertaken together with the commencement of restoration work with emphasis to the Hospital of the Knights. After its restoration it operated as a Museum (Regio Museo dello Spedale dei Cavalieri), which included a medieval section.[15] It is an undeniable fact that, irrespective of the early twentieth-century Italian conquerors' deeper motives, the monuments of the Hospitaller period were indeed looked after diligently and acquired to a great extent the condition in which we can encounter them today. It was not until the annexation of the Twelve Islands by the modern Greek state in 1948 that the Rhodian and other Dodecanesian monuments came under the jurisdiction and care of the local Ephorate of Byzantine Antiquities.

Contemporary Views on the Order of St John's History in Greece

A Greek journalist and writer well known for his monograph series on the history, topography and folklore of castles and fortresses in Greece, Yiannis Ghikas, offered the following interesting thoughts on his visit to the island of Cos and its castle:

> The shadows of the Grand Masters lie buried under the forgetfulness of the ruins and sealed in subterranean chambers that the axe of the archaeologist may never reveal; they do not venture to come out in the open, in order to face the peaceful reality, to scent the odor of the fresh herb and flower; they are eternally lost, interred in the trunk of illiteracy and indifference. Who would indeed be interested in them save those who 'scratch' historical writings and read about their past and glorious feats?[16]

We could say that the above extract – impressively vivid and at the same time painfully accurate – provides in a few bare lines the reality with which the Hospitaller past in the Dodecanese is nowadays generally viewed and understood in Greece. Truly, it looks as if the memory of the Knights of Saint John is kept alive only through the studies of historians and other scholars, while ceasing to exist in the collective memory of the Greek past. It is interesting to note here, in the form of a general observation, that despite the progress of modern Greek scholarship regarding the study of 'Latinocracy' in Greek lands after A.D. 1204, it is painfully evident that, for a significant section of modern Greek society, everything to do with the various facets of Latin domination in Byzantium's former lands is to be discarded and brushed aside.[17] Indicative of this tendency is the fact that in official Greek school textbooks there is minimal treatment of the Latin presence in Greek lands during the medieval and modern eras, while until quite recently several Latin medieval monuments lay in ruins completely unattended; however, this neglectful tendency has been at least partly ended in the case of archaeological finds.[18]

Particularly regarding the Knights Hospitaller, it is sadly the case that their memory on Rhodes and the rest of the Dodecanese is only faintly preserved.[19] The Rhodiots themselves seem to be painfully unaware about the Knights' history and presence on the island, while the only undeniable witness of their presence are the monuments themselves, which are mainly utilized in order to attract the attention of foreign visitors. The sole initiative to promote the Hospitaller past and thus bring the general public in closer contact with the island's medieval period belongs to the cultural association entitled 'Medieval Rose', which annually organizes the Medieval Festival of Rhodes. According to its organizers, however, this initiative has not been warmly embraced by the local population and it is treated, in the best of circumstances, with indifference – and often with suspicion, since it is associated with a historical period linked with Western conquerors and rulers, for whom the modern Greek subconscious does not maintain or harbour the best of reminiscences.[20]

This is a curious juxtaposition with the medieval past, if one takes into account the good relations which the Hospitallers maintained with the local Greek population in the course of their occupation of Rhodes and the Twelve Islands.[21] It is a characteristic fact that, when the order was forced to abandon Rhodes in early January of 1523, many Greek families decided to follow the Hospitallers and settled with them on Malta when that island was ceded to them in 1530.[22] Today, however, if we exclude the few readers of the relevant histories, it seems that this past is unknown and rather indifferent to the Rhodiots with the exception, of course, of those specialized researchers of history, archaeology and art history.

The attitude of modern Rhodiots poses a special interest compared to that on the part of the modern Maltese, who have indeed embraced their Hospitaller legacy. It is an interesting contradiction between two peoples who share a common page in their history. Maltese people view the Hospitallers as an important and crucial part of their history and this is totally understandable since, as we can firmly say, the presence of the order on the island of Malta formulated their identity. In Greece, however, the case is completely different, as the Greeks are coming from a distinctive past from which they had already shaped their identity, defined predominantly by their language and their Orthodox faith. Although in the course of Hospitaller rule they managed to live in peace and harmony, this fact was not enough to preserve the order's place in the collective memory.

Conclusions

On the basis of what we have said so far we are in a position to draw some conclusions regarding the preservation of memory as well as the perception with which the Knights of Saint John are viewed today in Greece. If we attempted to make an overall evaluation, we could say that the topic presents a variety of facets. Regarding the academic milieu, Greek scholars who have dealt with the Order's history are few in number although they have offered very notable contributions. A veritable desideratum would probably be the need for a dissemination of that particular historical knowledge to a wider public through a high-level popularization. On the other hand, concerning the care of the monuments and the development of archaeological research, it is evident that here we have significant results, especially if we take into account the limited financial resources that have perennially been afforded to the Humanities.

Yet, we cannot help but bewail the total alienation and lack of connection with this historical past among Greeks today, despite that past's importance, although such an indifference is perhaps to be expected in our time as it is associated with the image of 'the other', the image of 'the different'. Such a phenomenon, however, is provocative and deserves to be further investigated, since the intercultural interplay which was in force during the era of the rule of the Hospitallers on Rhodes and in the Dodecanese was of paramount importance; truly, that era's living remains are its impressive surviving monuments which we encounter rising proud and unassailable across the centuries.

Notes

1 A basic bibliography on the Order, in Ph. V. Perra, 'Hospitaller Knights', in *Encyclopaedic Prosopographical Lexicon of Byzantine History and Civilization (=EPLBHC)*, vol. 3 (Turnhour: Brepols, 2012), pp. 252–55.

2 In this case we shall refer only to Greek scholars, without however omitting some of the general contributions produced by eminent scholars of the international academic community.

3 On House Delenda, see D. Kasapides, 'Delenda, House', *EPLBHC* 2 (2008), pp. 323–24. Here I would like to thank Dr Demetrios Kasapides for valuable information concerning Ioannes Delendas' personality.

4 I. Delendas, *Οι Ιωαννίται Ιππόται της Ρόδου (του Αγίου Ιωάννου της Ιερουσαλήμ, της Ρόδου, της Μάλτας...)* (Athens, 1955).

5 *Ιστορία της Ρόδου από τους προϊστορικούς χρόνους έως την ενσωμάτωση της Δωδεκανήσου, 1948* (Athens, 1972 and 2nd edition, 1994), with useful appendices by Ioannes Chr. Papachristodoulou on Antiquity, by Elias Kollias on Archaeology and Art and Zacharias N. Tsirpanles on the Middle Ages and the Modern Period.

6 Cf. review of the 2nd ed. (in Greek) by A. Savvides, in *Νέα Εστία* 137, fasc. 1627 (1995), p. 549.

7 Cf. Ch. Papachristodoulou, 'Η θέσις των Ορθοδόξων της Ρόδου την εποχή των Ιπποτών', *Δωδεκανησιακή Επιθεώρησις* 2–4 (1948), pp. 78–80. Bosio's translation into Greek remains a desideratum among Greek researchers, yet the extent of the work renders this possibility somewhat difficult; some extracts have been also translated in my *Ο λέων εναντίον της ημισελήνου. Ο πρώτος βενετο-οθωμανικός πόλεμος και η κατάληψη του ελλαδικού χώρου, 1463–1479* (Athens: Papazesses Publications, 2009, pp. 224–50). On Papachristodoulou see the obituary compiled (in Greek) by D. Krekoukias, *Νέα Εστία* 125, fasc. 1480 (1989), p. 335.

8 Among his most valuable works are: *Οι Ιππότες της Ρόδου. Το Παλάτι και η Πόλη*, Athens 1991 (with English, French, German and Italian translations); *Η Μεσαιωνική Πόλη και το Παλάτι του Μεγάλου Μαγίστρου* (Athens, 1994) (also English edition, 1988).

9 On E. Kollias and his work, see Helen (Eleni) Papavasiliou, 'Η προσφορά του επίτιμου Εφόρου Αρχαιοτήτων Ηλία Κόλλια μέσα από τη βιβλιογραφική παρουσία της 4ης E.B.A.', *Βυζαντινός Δόμος* 16 (2007–2008), pp. 465–77; cf. eadem, 'Εργογραφία του Ηλία Κόλλια', *ΔΧΑΕ* 30 (2009), pp. 11–14. See also the obituary compiled (in Greek) by Z. Tsirpanles, in *Βυζ. Δόμος*, ό.π. pp. 479–82.

10 Cf. Z.N. Tsirpanles, *Ανέκδοτα έγγραφα για τη Ρόδο και τις Νότιες Σποράδες από το Αρχείο των Ιωαννιτών Ιπποτών 1421–1453*, vol. I (Rhodes: Ministry of Culture, 1995), with a prologue by E. Kollias and review (in Greek) by A. Savvides, *Βυζαντινός Δόμος* 8–9 (1995–97; publ. 1998), pp. 60–261 (the eagerly awaited v. II for the period 1454–1523 has not yet appeared). Several archival references are also encountered in his former collected studies volume entitled *Η Ρόδος και οι Νότιες Σποράδες στα χρόνια των Ιωαννιτών Ιπποτών (14ος-16ος αι.)* (Rhodes, 1991).

11 Για τον J. Hedenborg και το έργο του βλ. αναλυτικά Alexandra Stefanidou, *Η Μεσαιωνική Ρόδος με βάση το χειρόγραφο και την εικονογράφηση του Johannes Hedenborg (1854)* (Thessaloniki: Ant. Stamoules Publications, 2004).

12 On this, see Elias Kollias' introductory note in *Medieval Town of Rhodes. Restoration Works (1985–2000)*, Katerina Manoussou ed. (Rhodes, 2001), p. 14.

13 On this period, see the special contribution by Z.N. Tsirpanles, *Ιταλοκρατία στα Δωδεκάνησα 1912–1943*, Rhodes 1998, with a preface by Elias Kollias.

14 On this issue, see analytically by Tsirpanles, *Ιταλοκρατία*, pp. 90–92.

15 Tsirpanles, *Ιταλοκρατία*, p. 286, for the Italians' architectural interventions on Hospitaller monuments, see p. 287.

16 See Y. Ghikas, *Κάστρα-Ταξίδια στην Ελλάδα του θρύλου και της πραγματικότητας*, vol. 3 (Athens, 1985), p. 223.

17 On this, see the recent survey by A. Savvides, 'Σπουδές μεσαιωνικής ιστορίας στην Ελλάδα (δυτικής Ευρώπης-Λατινοκρατίας). Μεσαιωνολόγοι ιστορικοί ερευνητές του απώτατου και πρόσφατου παρελθόντος», *Βυζαντινός Δόμος* 27 (2019), pp. 1–33.

18 Such a realization is a common corollary encountered by the present author when she was a student, as well as through the experiences of today's students, who upon entering university studies are forced to confess that their knowledge on the Latin dominions in Greece during the Middle Ages and the Modern Period is quite limited, testifying to the continuing tradition of this phenomenon.

19 It was during a related query undertaken by Mr Pierros Demestichas, a student of the Department of History, Archaeology and Cultural Resources Management of Peloponnesos University, in his B.D. dissertation supervised by the present author, that both an illiteracy as well as an indifference on the part of the Rhodiots regarding the Hospitaller past of their island was plainly discerned through the posed questionnaire; the dissertation is currently in progress and its conclusions upon completion will add to this discussion.

20 For a general picture regarding Graeco-Latin relations and the ways in which Westerners were perceived by the Orthodox populations in medieval Greece, see my article 'Η εικόνα του άλλου κατά το Μεσαίωνα: Όψεις των σχέσεων μεταξύ Ελλήνων και Λατίνων (10ος-15ος αι.)', in *Πολιτισμός και διαφορετικότητα. Εμείς και οι άλλοι* (Thessalonica: Ant. Stamoules Publications, 2011), pp. 106–17. The topic of the overall perceptions of former Western dominations, as viewed in Modern Greece, is in itself a most interesting subject for further research.

21 On this, see the article by Anthony Luttrell, 'The Greeks of Rhodes under Hospitaller Rule', in his collected studies volume *The Hospitaller State on Rhodes and Its Western Provinces, 1306–1462* (London: Variorum Reprints, 1999), pp. 193–223; cf. Z.N. Tsirpanles, *Η Ρόδος και οι Νότιες Σποράδες, supra* (footnote 8).

22 See A. Savvides, ''Πόλεμος και διπλωματία: οι σχέσεις των Ιωαννιτών Ιπποτών της Ρόδου με τον μουσουλμανικό κόσμο (Τουρκομάνους, Μαμελούκους και Οθωμανούς)', in A. Savvides-N. Nikoloudes, *Ο ύστερος μεσαιωνικός κόσμος (11ος-16ος αι.)* (Athens: Hêrodotos, 2007), pp. 353–66, at 364–66; cf. my article 'Από την βυζαντινή στην ιπποτοκρατούμενη Ρόδο (αρχές 7ου-αρχές 16ου αι.): σελίδες από τη μεσαιωνική ιστορία του νοτιοανατολικού Αιγαίου', *Βυζαντινός Δόμος* 27 (2019), pp. 51–69, at 61–62.

Bibliography

Primary Sources

Medieval Town of Rhodes. Restoration Works (1985–2000). ed. Katerina Manoussou-Della. Rhodes: Ministry of Culture, 2001.

Tsirpanles, Z. N. *Ανέκδοτα έγγραφα για τη Ρόδο και τις Νότιες Σποράδες από το Αρχείο των Ιωαννιτών Ιπποτών 1421-1453*, vol. 1. Rhodes: Ministry of Culture, 1995.

Secondary Sources

Delendas, I. *Οι Ιωαννίται Ιππόται της Ρόδου (του Αγίου Ιωάννου της Ιερουσαλήμ, της Ρόδου, της Μάλτας...)*. Athens, 1955.

Ghikas, Y. *Κάστρα-Ταξίδια στην Ελλάδα του θρύλου και της πραγματικότητας*, vol. 3. Athens, 1985.

Kasapides, D. 'Delenda, House'. In A. Savvides and B. Hendrickx (eds), *Encyclopaedic Prosopographical Lexicon of Byzantine History and Civilization (=EPLBHC)*, vol. 2. Turnhout: Brepols, 2008, pp. 323–24.

Kolias, E. *Οι Ιππότες της Ρόδου. Το Παλάτι και η Πόλη*. Athens: Ekdotiki Athinon, 1991.

Luttrell, A. 'The Greeks of Rhodes under Hospitaller Rule'. In A. Luttrell (ed.), *The Hospitaller State on Rhodes and Its Western Provinces, 1306–1462*. London: Variorum Reprints, 1999, pp. 193–223.

Papachristodoulou, C. Ή θέσις των Ορθοδόξων της Ρόδου την εποχή των Ιπποτών'. *Δωδεκανησιακή Επιθεώρησις* 2–4 (1948), pp. 78–80.

Papavasiliou, H. (Eleni). Ή προσφορά του επίτιμου Εφόρου Αρχαιοτήτων Ηλία Κόλλια μέσα από τη βιβλιογραφική παρουσία της 4ης Ε.Β.Α.' *Βυζαντινός Δόμος* 16 (2007–2008), pp. 465–77.

———. 'Εργογραφία του Ηλία Κόλλια'. *ΔΧΑΕ* 30 (2009), pp. 11–14.

Perra, Ph. V. Ή εικόνα του άλλου κατά το Μεσαίωνα: Όψεις των σχέσεων μεταξύ Ελλήνων και Λατίνων (10ος-15ος αι.)'. In Magriplis G. Dimitrios (ed.), *Πολιτισμός και διαφορετικότητα. Εμείς και οι άλλοι*. Thessalonica: Ant. Stamoules Publications, 2011, pp. 106–17.

———. 'Hospitaller Knights'. In S. Lambakis (ed.), *EPLBH*, vol. 3. Turnhout: Brepols, 2012, pp. 252–55.

Savvides, A. ''Πόλεμος και διπλωματία: οι σχέσεις των Ιωαννιτών Ιπποτών της Ρόδου με τον μουσουλμανικό κόσμο (Τουρκομάνους, Μαμελούκους και Οθωμανούς)'. In A. Savvides and N. Nikoloudes (eds.). *Ο ύστερος μεσαιωνικός κόσμος (11ος-16ος αι.)*. Athens: Hêrodotos, 2007, pp. 353–66.

———. 'Σπουδές μεσαιωνικής ιστορίας στην Ελλάδα (δυτικής Ευρώπης-Λατινοκρατίας). Μεσαιωνολόγοι ιστορικοί ερευνητές του απώτατου και πρόσφατου παρελθόντος». *Βυζαντινός Δόμος* 27 (2019), pp. 1–33.

Stefanidou, A. *Η Μεσαιωνική Ρόδος με βάση το χειρόγραφο και την εικονογράφηση του Johannes Hedenborg (1854)*. Thessaloniki: Ant. Stamoules Publications, 2004.

Tsirpanles, Z. N. *Η Ρόδος και οι Νότιες Σποράδες στα χρόνια των Ιωαννιτών Ιπποτών (14ος-16ος αι.)*. Rhodes: Office of the Medieval City of Rhodes, 1991.

———. *Ιταλοκρατία στα Δωδεκάνησα 1912–1943*. Rhodes: Ministry of Culture, 1998.

5 Taking the Cross and Asserting Freedom

Catholic Liberalism, the Military Orders, and the Perception of the Crusades in Mexico in the First Half of the Nineteenth Century

Ignacio García Lascurain Bernstorff

This study analyzes the presence of members of the Iberian military orders and the depiction of the Crusades in Mexican literature as an aspect of Catholic liberal thought in Mexico in the nineteenth century. By 1840 there were a handful members of these military orders residing in Mexico. They were Classicist intellectuals and politicians, who espoused a moderate Catholic Liberalism in cultural debates, particularly the Knight of Montesa, José Justo Gómez de la Cortina († 1860), who wrote the only known Mexican piece about the Templars and held a public debate on the utility of learning the history of the Crusades in 1844. All these knights also had strong ties to Spain. As far as it is possible to determine from the sparse sources, their membership of these military orders was a remnant of their experiences in Spain.

Mexico and the Military Orders

In 1910, Antonio Rossi, writing the history of his Ligurian hometown Santo Stefano d'Aveto, claimed that the parish's painting of the Mexican Virgin of Guadalupe had been aboard the galley of Giovanni Andrea Doria († 1606), a prominent knight of Santiago, in the Battle of Lepanto on October 17, 1571.[1] One of the knight's descendants, Cardinal Giuseppe Maria Doria Pamphilij († 1816), had bestowed the painting in 1811 on Santo Stefano, one of the oldest fiefs of his family.[2] If Lepanto can be regarded under certain definitions as the last great Crusade battle – understood as a multinational endeavor under the guidance of the Papacy, usually against a Muslim opponent – then it is clear that the Crusades and Latin America, where European colonies

DOI: 10.4324/9781003200802-6

were still in their infancy in 1571, belong to different historical periods, having few entanglements other than this connection with Lepanto.[3]

However, the early incorporation of American societies into the West raises the question of the standing and presence of the military orders and of their 'genetic shibboleth', the Crusade, in nineteenth-century Mexico. Following the distinction made by Jonathan Riley-Smith, scholarship has shown that both the military-religious orders 'proper' – such as the Hospitallers of St. John and the Teutonic Knights – and the so-called Christian chivalric orders (the five Iberian military orders, but also the Tuscan Order of St. Stephen and even the Order of the Golden Fleece) carried the notion of Crusade into the Early Modern Period.[4] It is in this tenor that this study explores the memory of the military orders in nineteenth-century Mexico. This chapter shall show that, in the middle of this period, the original Iberian military orders disappeared completely from the country, replaced by a new Mexican order that positioned itself as their heir. At the same time, a diffuse awareness of the Crusades entrenched the earlier military orders in popular memory.

The presence of the military orders in Mexico has seen very little study. In the early twentieth century, amateur historians compiled lists of members of the orders but without citing their sources.[5] The scattered nature of the sources remains difficult. There is no single central public archive (either state or ecclesiastical) holding this information.[6] Departing from this limited historiography, which underlined the paramount role played by the creation, or at least proposal, of 'military orders' inspired by the Spanish orders as an instrument of fostering the creation of a national identity for newly independent Mexico, this present study may shed some light on this largely unexplored field by discussing three understudied sources: the '*Canto a los Caballeros Guadalupanos*' (1855) of the printer Santiago Pérez, the short essay *Los Templarios* (1829/1840) by the Knight of Montesa José Justo Gómez de la Cortina († 1860), as well as a letter regarding the departure of a Knight of Malta from Mexico in the early 1840s.

A Difficult Spanish Heritage

The military orders were never prominent in the Early Modern New World. One can still ask, as the Quebecois notary Joseph-Edmond Roy († 1913) did, why such vibrant communities did not 'come to the American forests' and 'add great and beautiful pages to their already glorious history'.[7] While geopolitics may explain the complete absence of the Teutonic Knights, the sparse presence of the Order of Malta and even of the Spanish military orders, the latter by then subordinated to the crown, is striking. There were certainly structural problems. The failed proposal for an autonomous Mexican Maestranza (aristocratic militia) in 1790, despite Mexico having a considerable number of nobles in the last decades of the eighteenth century – both born in the New World and in Spain – was one of two major factors which impeded the flourishing and/or establishment of the military orders until the middle of the twentieth century.[8] The other factor or, rather, event was the mass expulsion of Spaniards from Mexico ordered in March 1829, after an earlier unsuccessful attempt in December 1827.[9] The expulsion forced the members of the aristocracy (from which the ranks of the military orders were recruited) to make a political decision: to go into exile or to definitively end collective forms of organization and action related to the Crown. Between 1827 and 1829 about 7,000 Spaniards left Mexico, mostly sailing first to New Orleans, from where they dispersed to other cities, especially Philadelphia, New York, Marseille, and Bayonne.[10] Numerically speaking, the biggest role of the Military Orders before Mexican Independence was probably in the posting of the infantry regiment 'Órdenes Militares' to Mexico between 1815 and 1821. This regiment had been created by the four Spanish military orders in response to Spain's participation in the anti-French War of the First Coalition (1793–97); the regiment was financed by the revenues of the orders' commanderies.[11] With the exception of some officers, the soldiers were not themselves members of the orders.

Still, recent historiography has underlined the lasting heritage of the military orders in Mexico through the creation of Mexican secular orders – especially the Order of Guadalupe, which defined itself as a Catholic 'military order'.[12] If it is true that the Spanish military orders, after their secularization in the sixteenth century, developed into 'social capital tools', in the words of Bourdieu, which fulfilled the integration of the élites (new and old) of the Spanish Empire into the Monarchy, it is worth asking whether these Mexican order(s) – only the Order of Guadalupe was actually created before the twentieth century – were really inspired by the old Spanish military orders rather than by other models such as France's 1802 Legion of Honour or Spain's Order of Charles III from the 1770s (itself also defined as a military order).[13]

The Illustrious and Distinguished Order of Our Lady of Guadalupe: Three Attempts at Creating an Autochthonous Military Order

Already in 1812, in the middle of the Mexican War of Independence, the lawyer, general, and independence leader Ignacio López Rayón (†1832) proposed in his *Elementos Constitucionales* the creation of four

Mexican military orders: the Military Order of Our Lady of Guadalupe, the Military Order of Hidalgo, the Military Order of the Eagle, and the Military Order of Allende. The number four being a reference to the four Spanish military orders of Santiago, Calatrava, Alcántara, and Montesa. Of these proposed creations, only the Order of Guadalupe was created.[14] On February 20, 1822, the junta ruling Mexico prior to the coronation of Emperor Augustin of Mexico († 1824) approved the statues of the National and Distinguished Order of Guadalupe. Members were to be divided into three classes, without distinction between military and civilians (just between ecclesiastics and lay men): Knight Grand Crosses, Numerary Knights, and Super-numerary Knights. The Order was intended to be a purely meritocratic one, recognizing the dedication and merits of individual citizens.[15] In both these respects, the Order of Guadalupe reproduced the model of the Order of Charles III, created in 1771, and which had exactly the same grades since it was first reformed in 1778.[16] However, whereas the Order of Charles III required that knights have *limpieza de sangre* going back four generations on each side (but not noble ancestry), the Order of Guadalupe did not require this.[17] In this sense, the Order of Guadalupe took the democratic paradigm of the Legion of Honour. Throughout its history, the order's medal has been an oval in the middle of a cross, with the Virgin of Guadalupe on the front and the inscription '*Religión, Independencia, Unión*' on the reverse. In the first incarnation of the order, the cross was a rudimentary petal cross, whereas in the second and third incarnations, it was a cross pattée. Across all three creations, the Order was to be guided by the grand master, together with the grand chancellor, the fiscal (overseeing the internal regulations of the order), and the 'clavero', literally the Key-Holder, overseeing the finances. With every new incarnation of the order, the number of members was changed. In March 1823 the order ceased to exist for the first time with the abdication of the emperor and the proclamation of the First Republic.

On November 11, 1853, one of the former Grand Crosses of this first order, General Antonio López de Santa-Anna († 1876), recreated it as the acting President of Mexico. The aforementioned José Justo Gómez de la Cortina was the *spiritus rector* of the reestablishment, organizing the protocol, some of the important events, and the uniforms.[18] The whole project was intended to create a corporation of Christian knights serving the nation, as recorded in his 1829 essay *Idea general de la caballería*, printed in his *Cartilla histórica*.

The restored order showed the consolidation of the country in those years, dominated by moderate Liberals striving for a republican system reconciled with the Catholic Church, yet at the same time proud of its roots in the French Revolution.[19] Pope Pius IX approved the statutes on April 4, 1854, and almost every head of state of the European countries which had diplomatic relations with the young republic received the Grand Cross of the Order, regardless of their confession, including Emperor Napoleon III, Queen Victoria, Queen Isabella II of Spain, and the Prussian King Frederick William IV. According to the fashionable new organization of the military orders from the 1840s onward, a new division of ranks inspired by the Legion of Honour was introduced: members were now to be Knight Grand Cross, Knight Commander, or Knight. The grand master was the president himself, who used the titles '*Benémerito de la Patria, General de División, Caballero Gran Cruz de la Real y Distinguida Orden Española de Carlos III, Presidente de la República Mexicana*' reflecting both his military career since the War of Independence (thus *Benémerito de la Patria*, as were all other officers who signed the Act of Independence) and his conciliatory policy toward Spain.[20] Remarkably in this new creation, a bond with other orders and a lineage with the military orders of the crusades were asserted, as shown in two brief sources.

On December 20, 1854, there was a festive thanksgiving commemorating the first anniversary of the reestablishment of the Order. At eight o'clock a stately procession began from the National Palace (the 'residence of the grand master') in Mexico City to the Metropolitan Cathedral, located some 300 meters to the north. The procession, which included virtually all senior governmental officials, moved slowly under large canopies, in the midst of honor guards of grenadiers, and with bands playing in the background parallel to gun salutes. Upon arriving at the Cathedral, the knights placed themselves according to their status. At the right of the high altar, directly by the episcopal throne, the president – as grand master – took his place, together with his family. Opposite, to the left of the altar, the organizer of the ceremony, the commissioner of the municipal government of Mexico City José Algara y Gómez († 1867) had placed two balconies: one destined for the Diplomatic Corps and another 'for the knights of foreign Orders'.[21] In the latter were the prominent educator and former minister José María Lacunza († 1869), Knight Grand Cross of the Order of Pope Pius IX (the Pian Order), Juan Manuel de Lasquetty, Commander of the Order of Charles III and scion of a prominent merchant dynasty from Cádiz, the brothers and architects Juan and Ramón Agea, representing the 'Italian [sic!] Order of Saint Gregory' and Vicente de Iturrigaray y Jáuregui († 1869), Knight of the Order of Malta. José Justo Gómez was also there, standing at the entrance of the choir. He was also the leader of the 'Commission of the Foreign Orders', which acted as an advisory board at this creation of the Order of Guadalupe.[22] Both Lacunza and Iturrigaray will play a role in the following pages.

The presence there of both Iturrigaray and Gómez shows that clearly the distinction of Riley-Smith between military and chivalric orders did not apply in the conception of the military orders in Mexico. In the notion '*Órdenes Militares*' the Mexicans understood this to mean Christian-inspired merit orders concentrating the notables of a particular country, rather than a military-religious institution of members bound by professed vows living under a monastic rule. In the case of the Order of Malta, this judgment was neither completely wrong for the circumstances of the time (as will be shown later) nor even a local peculiarity.[23] The Order of Guadalupe was a military order, again following in the steps of the Order of Charles III, simply by self-definition.

A year later, it became clear that the new Mexican order was not just on good terms with other chivalric orders, but that it saw itself as emulating the medieval military orders. The 88-page booklet *Calendario nuevo de los Cruzados de la Nacional y Distinguida Orden Guadalupana, promovida y establecida por el libertador de la patria Don Agustín de Iturbide el año de 1822 y restaurada por su alteza serenísima, benemérito de la patria, general presidente Antonio López de Santa-Anna el año de 1853* by Santiago Pérez is divided into three parts: first, a meteorological, civic, and religious calendar (up to p. 28); second, a general introduction to the Order of Guadalupe with its statues, ceremonial, and a list of its members (pp. 29–52); and third, a poem entitled 'Song to the Guadalupean Knights' ('*Canto a los Caballeros Guadalupanos*'). Already the name of the publication, 'New calendar of the Crusaders of the National and Distinguished Guadalupean Order, fostered [...] in the year 1853', suggests an ideological range uniting the crusades with the newly self-denominated military order. This is partially true since *Cruzados* comes from 'cruzar' (cfr. Article 5 of the statues), meaning both entering into a military order and taking the cross.

The 'Song' makes these links even more explicit. The poem is divided into five parts. It praises the resurrection of the order and invites the knights to commit themselves to it. Whereas the second and the third parts complain about the difficult political and social situation in Mexico, the fourth part recounts the recreation of 1853, before stressing the commitment of the new knights in the last part. The first part situates the Order of Guadalupe in a direct descent from the medieval military orders. The first verses recall the hierarchy of the order and the desolate situation of the country, where, however, hope has begun to grow. As was already done in 1822 in the first establishment of the order, Mexicans are identified with the Aztecs to whom 'Europe without pride extends its strong hand'.[24] After 30 years of chaos, and the 'dishonor' of having lost the Mexican-American War (1846–48), the new Knights promise a new era, because

> You are the successors, Mexican Knights, of the brave warriors, of the illustrious Crusaders who went to conquer the holy banners which had been usurped by the fierce Saracens in Palestine. Remember Godfrey, the great Pontiff Urban, Francis the king of France and the intrepid Richard. Remember Count Stephen, Emperor Eustace, Robert, Philip, Augustus, Hugh the Great and many others. Remember the Order of Malta, the Teutonic and the Templars, and the pious institution which was Saint Lazarus. All these knights, for Peter, the great hermit, for the holy Religion took the sword. And a thousand good deeds were done strenuously in everyplace they were; everywhere they passed by.
>
> The Knights of Malta, always with joy and pleasure, extended their hands upon every pauper. Those of the Teutonic Order busily aided every kind of sick person who did not have shelter. With religious zeal the Templar Knights guarded the trails of the Holy Land at every hour. And with great love those of Saint Lazarus took care of the lepers without showing any grief.
>
> They were knights of high esteem that were decorated for their heroic deeds. All of them sustained their great sovereigns, following their dispositions with obedient submission.[25]

Here, the song's author, Santiago Pérez, shows an awareness of the military orders as entities that fostered national integration and unity, as the Spanish military orders did in the New World. His knowledge of crusade history has some errors, including the mysterious 'Francis the king of France'. This was most probably from his reading Michaud's *Histoire des Croisades* (1812–22), first published in Spanish in 1831, as shown by the emphasis that Pérez places upon French Crusades such as Hugh of Vermandois († 1101), Stephen of Blois († 1102), and Eustace of Hainaut († 1216). In 'Francis king of France', Pérez probably referred to Francis I († 1547), whose chivalric and crusade ethos is praised by Michaud, together with Charlemagne.[26] Pérez probably also knew the popular compendium *La Tierra Santa* (1842), which just mentioned the military orders, without specifying their activities.[27] His knowledge of them is drawn from the proposal for new military orders made in the writings of José Justo Gómez de la Cortina.

The second iteration of the Order came to an abrupt end when President Santa-Anna, trying to mitigate the consequences of the Revolution of Ayutla, a series of Liberal revolts beginning in February 1855, dissolved the order in October 1855.[28] On June 30, 1863, however, the order was recreated yet again by a new junta, shortly before the creation of the Second Mexican Empire. On April 10, 1865, the chosen Emperor, Maximilian von Hapsburg, turned the order from a military order following the model of the Order of Charles III into a merely civic order, definitively ending this chapter of the revival of the military orders in Mexico.[29]

The 'Classic' Military Orders in Nineteenth-Century Mexico – Between Historical Studies and Reality

How did a 'normal Mexican intellectual', such as Santiago Pérez, experience the 'classic' military orders? We shall begin with a look at the Order of Malta, present at the event of 1854, and at the Spanish military orders, before moving on to a popular text on the Templars.

Apart from their brief possession of the Lesser Antilles between 1651 and 1665 and some individual knights who acted as colonial administrators in New France in the seventeenth century and in Spanish America in the eighteenth century, the Order of Malta had little presence in the Americas. In Mexico, there were just two examples of Hospitaller Knights acting as colonial administrators prior to independence in 1821: the Governor of Yucatán from 1670 to 1672 fra' Fernando Escobedo († 1688) and Baillif fra'Antonio María de Bucareli y Ursúa († 1779), Viceroy of New Spain from 1771 until his death. In 1946, Leopoldo Martínez Cosio listed in *Los Caballeros de las Órdenes Militares en México* another 12 Hospitallers living in the territory from the sixteenth to the eighteenth century, alas some of them with the dubious remark 'I do not know whom his parents/ancestors were, as also the date and place of his investiture' or 'the sole notice that I have is…'.[30]

The absence of the Order of Malta, which would continue with almost no interruption until the twentieth century, is to be explained by geopolitics. First, the American continent was too far from the two main fronts of the order's political activities: the war against the Barbary States and Europe's royal courts (especially those of the Bourbons and Hapsburgs) – where generations of Hospitallers cultivated a balance between protecting the order's interests and loyalty to their local monarchs. In the first half of the eighteenth century, the Spanish Crown had renewed its steady interventions in the order after almost a century of little interference, appointing all successive priors in Spain from among the scions of the royal family, culminating with the formal incorporation to the Crown of the order in Spain in January 1802, a situation which would last until 1885.[31] Second, this closeness to the Spanish Crown became more problematic with the independence of Mexico, particularly after the 1830s, when leading Mexican cultural voices, especially in the Church, decidedly cut ties with Spain.[32]

Albeit there were a few knights of Malta closely linked to Mexico in the first decades of this new nation. Mirroring the situation in Spain, where a growing number of new Knights of Grace (created since the secularization of the order as an award for services to the Crown) co-existed with a steadily smaller number of members from the pre-1802 annexation, the Mexican knights of Malta were the survivors of the leading élite of the final four decades of the Viceroyalty: mining and trade barons as well politicians, both recently ennobled and not, born in Mexico itself or emigrated at a young age and usually moving between Mexico and Spain repeatedly due to the political instability of the country.[33] The investiture was usually performed in Europe. One of the earliest examples is the second Count of La Valenciana, Antonio de Obregón y de la Barrera († 1833), a mining magnate who received royal appointment as a Knight of Grace of the Order of Malta in 1807.[34] Another knight, possibly one of the many knights created during the reign of Isabella II of Spain, was the aforementioned Vicente de Iturrigaray, second son of the former Viceroy José de Iturrigaray y Aróstegui († 1815), who left Mexico in 1843 together with his brother José after almost 30 years and was invested as knight of the Order in February 1852.[35] Vicente's portrait, reproduced below, shows this Paris-dwelling Spanish gentleman with strong ties to Mexico wearing his insignia of the Order of Santiago (1851) sewn onto his jacket and a Maltese cross hanging from a chain on his lapel together with an unidentified medal.[36] Though he is not recorded in the extensive *Índice de pruebas*, his investiture might be recorded in an uncertain entry in a list published in 2002 (Figure 5.1).[37]

The aforementioned José Justo Gómez de la Cortina was the most productive and prominent representative of the other Spanish orders in the country after independence. As a part of his literary work, he made the greatest contribution to the historical study of the military orders in Mexico in this period.[38]

Sent together with his brother to Madrid in 1815, he eventually graduated from the Academy of Alcalá and joined the diplomatic service. On May 14, 1828 he was created a Knight of Montesa.[39] His

Figure 5.1 Portrait of Vicente Iturrigaray, hand-colored salted paper print, 22.5 cm × 16.5 cm [8.85 × 6.49 inch], Paris, ca. 1853, Mayer frères, Mexico City, private collection.

appointment to Montesa, and not to the other Orders, appears to be related to his membership in the *Real Sociedad Económica de Amigos del País de Valencia*, as the medieval order was headquartered in the kingdom of Valencia. In 1832 he returned to Mexico, where he was elected to Congress as a representative, and in 1835 as a governor of the capital. Later, Gómez de la Cortina was Minister of Finance and again governor of Mexico City. In 1848, he ended his political career when he renounced Mexican citizenship in order to hold his inherited title of Count de la Cortina. Alongside his political career he founded the Mexican Geographical Society in 1833 and, two years later, the 'Language Academy', as well as serving as editor of the literary paper *El Zurriago Literario.* He died impoverished in 1860.

During his time in Madrid, he published *Cartilla histórica o método para estudiar la historia* in 1829.[40] From 1840, the work was reprinted many times in Mexico.[41] Both in chronology and scope, it stands between Voltaire's († 1778) *Essai sur les mœurs et l'espirit des nations* from 1756 and Dana Carleton Munro's († 1933) *Syllabus of Medieval History* from 1902.[42] The volume is also part of a tradition with the paramount classical lecture of Catholic World History from before the late-nineteenth century, Jacques-Bénigne de Bossuet's († 1704) *Discours sur l'histoire universelle* (1681), even though Gómez criticized its pedagogical value in an 1844 debate with José María Lacunza.[43] With the Cartilla, Gómez wanted to provide a new handbook for understanding the general dynamics and most important events of world history, beginning with an introduction on the nature of history, followed by 13 short essays. In this work, which he dedicated to the directors of his former school, he dubbed the crusades the fifth epoch of mankind. He dealt with the crusades after his account of the great empires of Antiquity and before the notion of chivalry, which Gómez saw as a creation of Carolingian Europe. Directly after chivalry, Gómez discussed Feudal Government and immediately after that, the Templars.

In his essay on the Templars, he quoted Bossuet ('*No se sabe, dice Bossuet*') regarding the prosecution of this order.[44] Gómez's account of this order is not to be seen primarily within the instrumentalization of Templar history, especially in France, since the early nineteenth century.[45] Instead, with his perspective, Gómez was a cause rather than a product for the historiographical 'legend' of this extinguished military order.[46] It was also not a product of Medievalist Romanticism, which had reached Mexico in the early 1840s with the popular play by Fernando Calderón († 1845) '*Herman o la Vuelta del Cruzado*' (1842).[47] Most probably Gómez underlined the importance the Templars, because his own Military Order, Montesa, was created out of their former estates in the Kingdom of Valencia. For a Knight of Montesa it was evident that the Templars were an existential milestone in history.[48]

Conclusion

The military orders had little physical presence in Mexico in the nineteenth century. The Spanish military orders, an important part of the colonial aristocracy, had vanished almost completely by 1850, together with scarcer ones like the Order of Malta. Nevertheless, the memory of the orders was cultivated in the new country and through the study of the Crusades, as elsewhere in the Western world, there was an awareness of the origins of the military orders.

The 'meritocratization' of the military orders, seeing these knights primarily as examples of virtue, helped maintain the memory of the orders in Mexico during Catholic Liberalism's political dominance from the 1830s to the late 1850s. This was palpable in the many incarnations of the Illustrious and Distinguished Order of Guadalupe, especially of 1853, which was modeled upon the 'last' Spanish military order, the Order of Charles III.

Both the reception of the historiography of the crusades and the creation of this Mexican military order involved members of other military-religious orders, particularly José Justo Gómez de la Cortina. Despite Mexico's independence, there remained an enduring personal link with the old military orders and a transatlantic transfer of ideas.

Notes

1 According to tradition, the Virgin of Guadalupe appeared in the outskirts of Mexico City in December 1531 to the Aztec convert Juan Diego Cuathlatoatzin († 1548), remaining then as an *archeropoietos* stamped in his coat. Years later the Archbishop of Mexico produced a copy of the coat for King Philip II, who gave it to Doria, hence the legend recorded by Rossi.

2 Rossi, *La Beata Vergine di Guadalupe e S. Stefano d'Aveto. Note e documenti.* Chiavari: Tipografia Artistica Colombo, 1910, p. 70. Rossi's work is analysed in Stagno: 'Immacolata india. L'immagine della Vergine di Guadalupe messicana a Genova e in Liguria', p. 383.

3 For Lepanto as the 'last battle of the Crusades', see Kenneth Setton, *The Papacy and the Levant*, IV, p. 1099.

4 Riley-Smith: 'Towards a History of Military-Religious Orders', p. 271. On military and mendicant orders, especially the Hospitallers of St. John and the Franciscans, as a living memory of medieval Outremer as late as the Enlightenment, see Allen: 'Upholding Tradition: Benedict XIV and the Hospitaller Order of St. John of Jerusalem at Malta, 1740–1758', p. 20.

5 These three works are almost all the historiography that exists regarding the presence of the Military Orders in Mexico: Romero de Terreros y Vinent: 'Las Órdenes Militares en México' in *Anales del Museo Nacional de Arqueología, Historia y Etnografía* (1912, 16, IV), pp. 199–235; Martínez Cosío, *Los Caballeros de las Órdenes Militares en México* (Mexico City, 1946); Editorial Santiago and León de la Barra, *Órdenes y Honores Pontificios en México* (Mexico City: Librería Urbe, 1957).

6 For example, the Mexican Association of the Order of Malta's archive only dates from the 1950s.

7 'Pourquoi cette ilustre compagnie, jetée come une sentinelle au milieu de la Méditerrannée, et qui défendit pendant trois cents ans les côtes d'Europe contre les invasions de la barberie, ne serait-elle pas venue dans les fôrets d'Amerique proteger les établissements chrétiens contre les ataques des infidèles? Quelles grandes et belles pages aurait ajoutées à son histoire déja si glorieuse', in Roy, *L'Ordre de Malte en Amérique*, p. 23. Roy also proved that the order's slight presence in New France had completely vanished by 1681 (p. 59).

8 Liehr, *Sozialgeschichte Spanischer Adelskorporationen. Die Maestranzas de Caballería* (1670–1808), pp. 78–80. For example, in 1808 there were living 19 members of the Real Maestranza de Ronda in Mexico City, cfr. *ad passim*, p. 136.

9 Krebs Wilckens, *La Iglesia de América Latina en el siglo XIX*, p. 96.

10 Ruiz de Gordejuela Urquijo, *La expulsión de los españoles de México y su destino incierto*, p. 120. From New York, a large part of the refugees returned to Europe and settled in Bordeaux, especially merchants from Mexico City with Basque origins, *ad passim*, pp. 124–25.

11 'Real Consejo de las Ordenes Militares. Hermanamiento Militar', https://www.ordenesmilitares.es/real-consejo/hermanamiento/ [accessed March 17, 2021].

12 Cruz Barney, 'Las Órdenes Militares en los Elementos Constitucionales de Ignacio López Rayón. Derecho premial en el movimiento insurgente de 1810', pp. 4–5; Borja Martínez, *Ilustre y distinguida Orden de Nuestra Señora de Guadalupe*, p. 9, Zárate Toscano, 'Tradición y modernidad: la Orden Imperial de Guadalupe, su organización y rituales', p. 193.

13 Created in 1771, the *Real y Muy Distinguida Orden de Carlos III*, was aimed to praise, as its motto said, the 'virtues and merits' of individual subjects.

14 In April 1865 Emperor Maximilian of Mexico († 1867) created the Imperial Order of the Mexican Eagle, which ceased to exist just two years later. The current Mexican Order of the Aztec Eagle was erected in 1933. Finally, the 'Miguel Hidalgo Award' was created in 1975, prescinding of the designation 'Order'.

15 The nationalist character of the order was explicitly expressed in its investiture ceremony. The candidate promised (1) to profess the Catholic faith, (2) to defend the independence of the country, its territory and laws, (3) not to collaborate in projects against the nation, (4) to obey the grand master, (5) to take care of the poor and sick members of the order, (6) to regard the other members as brothers.

16 In 1847 the order was reformed, being then organized into Grand Crosses, Effective Commanders, Commanders, and Knights. On the meritocratic novelty of the Order of Charles III, within the landscape of the military orders in Spain, cfr. Ceballos-Escalera y Gila, *La Real y Distinguida Orden Española de Carlos III*, p. 28.

17 On the *limpieza de sangre*, i.e., the proving of Old Christian ancestry (in contrast to Jewish /Muslim convert origin), cfr. Hering Torres, *Rassismus in der Vormoderne*.

18 Borja Martínez, *Ilustre y distinguida Orden*, pp. 53–55.

19 Fernández Fernández, 'El Liberalismo Católico en la prensa mexicana de la primera mitad del siglo XIX', *Historia*, 1:396 (2014), p. 63.

20 López de Santa-Anna's style was 'Well-esteemed of the Fatherland, Lieutenant General, Knight Grand Cross of the Royal and Distinguished Spanish Order of Charles III, President of the Mexican Republic'. He was appointed as Knight Grand Cross of Charles III on July 15, 1843, cfr. Ceballos-Escalera y Gila, *La Real y Distinguida Orden*, p. 259.

21 A considerable number of the diplomats were also members of the order, including the British Chargé d'affaires Percy William Doyle († 1887), Apostolic Delegate Monsignor Luigi Clementi († 1869), and his auditor at the Legation, Monsignor Ernesto Colognesi, who later would become one of the leading figures in Mexico's uneasy relationship with the Papacy. Article 6 of the order's statues also considered the invitation of members of foreign orders living in Mexico.

22 Borja Martínez, *Ilustre y distinguida Orden*, pp. 63–66. Borja Martínez edited the text of the anonymous *Historia de la Orden Mexicana de Nuestra*

Señora de Guadalupe (Mexico City: Imprenta del Correo de España, 1854). For Juan Argea, s. León de la Barra: Honores Pontificios, p. 84.

23 Cfr. e.g. Gritzner, *Handbuch der Ritter- und Verdienstorden aller Kulturstaaten der Welt innerhalb des XIX. Jahrhunderts*, pp. 532–33.

24 '*Pues los míseros aztecas/Tras penas y horribles daños* [...] *Pues México se nivela/Con las naciones de rango./ Ya la Europa sin orgullo/ Le tiende su fuerte mano*', p. 54. For the identification of the knights with Aztec warriors, s. Zárate Toscano: La Orden de Guadalupe, p. 211.

25 '*Porque vos sois los sucesores/Caballeros mexicanos,/De los valientes guerreros, /De los ínclitos cruzados/ Que fueron a conquistar/ Los pendones sacrosantos,/ Que los fieros sarracenos/ En Palestina usurparon. Recordad a Godofredo,/ Al gran pontífice Urbano,/ A Francisco rey de Francia, / Y al intrépido Ricardo./ Recordad al conde Estéban,/ Al emperador Eustaquio,/ Roberto, Felipe, Augusto/ Hugo el Grande y otros varios:/ Recordad la Orden de Malta,/ La Teutónica y Templarios, Y la institución piadosa/ De la que fue San Lázaro./ Todos estos caballeros/ por Pedro, el grande ermitaño,/ Por la santa religión/ Sus espadas empuñaron. Y mil obras de piedad/ Practicaban afanados/ En donde quiera que estaban,/ Do quiera que iban de paso. Los Caballeros de Malta/ siempre con placer y agrado/ Sobre cualquier desvalido/ Estendían su franca mano:/ Los de la Teutónica Orden/ Auxiliaban afanados, / A toda clase de enfermos/ Que no tuvieran amparo. Todos ellos sostenían/ A sus grandes soberanos,/ Las disposiciones de éstos/ Con sumisión atacando*': Pérez, *Calendario nuevo de los Cruzados*, pp. 54–55. Also printed in Borja, *Orden de Guadalupe*, pp. 70–71.

26 Michaud, *Histoire des Croisades*, chap. VIII.

27 Galván Rivera, *Mariano: La Tierra Santa* (Mexico City, 1842).

28 Borja, *Orden de Guadalupe*, p. 79.

29 Ibid., p. 101.

30 Leopoldo Martínez Cosío, *Los Caballeros de las Órdenes Militares*, pp. 333–35. Eight out of the 13 Hospitallers bear these remarks. Lohmann Villena, *Los Americanos en las Órdenes Nobiliarias*, vol. I, p. LXXVII counts even just seven knights of Malta in Latin America.

31 Roberto Quirós Rosado, 'Estratégicos anacronismos. Malta, la Orden de San Juan y la Corona española a fines del Antiguo Régimen (1795–1802)', p. 129. In July 1847, the order was even transformed by Royal Decree into a mere 'civil decoration' with a maximum of 200 members, cfr. Carlos Nieto Sánchez, 'De la Ínclita Orden de San Juan de Jerusalén a la Asamblea Española: evolución de la Orden de Malta desde el siglo XIX hasta la actualidad', p. 495.

32 Sergio Francisco Rosas Salas, 'Defender la independencia y soberanía de la Iglesia: El perfil del primer episcopado mexicano a través de Francisco Pablo Vázquez y Juan Cayetano Gómez de Portugal', p. 57; Ricardo Krebs Wilckens, *La Iglesia*, p. 172 and Zárate Toscano, *La Orden de Guadalupe*, p. 208.

33 Nieto Sánchez, *De la Ínclita Orden de San Juan de Jerusalén a la Asamblea Española*, p. 499.

34 Carlos Nieto Sánchez and Jaime de Salazar Acha, 'Caballeros de gracia españoles en la Orden de Malta (1802–1808)', p. 418.

35 They left Mexico on May 15, 1829, following the expulsion of the Spaniards on March 19, 1829, cfr. Jesús Ruiz de Gordejuela Urquijo, *La expulsion de los españoles de México*, p. 310. They settled in Philadelphia. On November 24, 1829, President Vicente Guerrero († 1831) allowed their

return to Mexico at the insistence of their mother, cfr. Maria Graciela León Matamoros, 'El desamparo como argumento: mujeres en defensa de padres, esposos e hijos ante la ley de expulsión de españoles de 1829 en México', https://doi.org/10.4000/alhim.3160 [accessed March 17, 2021].

36 He was invested as a Knight of Santiago at Cádiz in 1851, cfr. Vicente Vignau and Francisco Uhagón (eds.), *Índice de pruebas de los caballeros que han vestido el hábito de Santiago desde el año 1501 hasta la fecha*, p. 176.

37 Alfonso Pardo y Manuel de Villena and Fernando Suárez de Tangil y de Angulo, *Índice de pruebas de los caballeros que han vestido el hábito de San Juan de Jerusalén (Orden de Malta) en el Gran Priorato de Castilla y León desde 1514 hasta la fecha*, p. 73 (Iturrigaray with I) and p. 161 (Yturrigaray with Y). Alfonso de Ceballos-Escalera y Gila *et al.*, *La Orden de Malta en España (1802–2002)*, p. 108.

38 For a bibliography concerning José Justo Gómez de la Cortina, see Francisco Miguel Espino Jiménez, 'José Justo Gómez de la Cortina y Gómez de la Cortina', http://dbe.rah.es/biografias/82136/jose-justo-gomez-de-la-cortina-y-gomez-de-la-cortina [accessed February 27, 2021]. His brother, the Marquis of Morante Joaquín Gómez de la Cortina y Gómez de la Cortina († 1868), was invested as a Knight of Santiago on January 28 1848. Regarding the awarded with the Santiago Cross in late Viceregal Mexico, it's important to take into account that the dynastic change of the Spanish monarchy to the Bourbon line in the early 18th century drastically reduced appointments to this order, dropping to almost a third of that of the last decades of Habsburg rule, cfr. Liehr, *Sozialgeschichte Spanischer Adelskorporationen*, p. 328.

39 Vincente Cadenas y Vicent, *Caballeros de Montesa que efectuaron sus pruebas de ingreso durante el siglo XIX*, p. 119.

40 *Cartilla moral o método para estudiar la Historia* (Madrid: Eusebio Aguado, 1829).

41 The reprint made by Ignacio Cumplido in Mexico City in 1840.

42 On Munro's importance for the historiography of the Crusades in North America, cfr. Hans Eberhard Mayer, 'America and the Crusades', pp. 39–40.

43 Juan Antonio Ortega y Medina, 'Discurso y cartas sobre varias reformas que parece deben hacerse en el método de algunos de nuestros estudios científicos. Polémica epistolar entre José Gómez de la Cortina y José María Lacunza', p. 138.

44 Bossuet's narrative on the Templars is repeated by Gómez: the Templars were established in the crusades, were good and meritorious, then their donations corrupted them. Philip IV of France, more moved by his greed than fearing the mighty and corrupted knights, plotted against the Templars. Then follows an original piece of Gómez's: he explains the basic structures of the order, the reception ceremony, and the order's banner.

45 Philippe Josserand: 'The Templar Order in Public and Cultural Debate in France during the Eighteenth and Nineteenth centuries', p. 148.

46 Kristijan Toomaspoeg, 'Die Geschichtsschreibung zu den mittelalterlichen geistlichen Ritterorden: status quaestionis', p. 31.

47 This play masterfully shows the values of Catholic Liberalism, stressing the personal freedom and merit of the crusader Hernán, together with his fidelity and strong religiosity. In the play he returns from the Second Crusade to marry his beloved lady in a German castle. After the strenuous opposition of her father, the duke, it comes out that Hernán is actually his

illegitimate son. Everyone is reconciled and Hernán then returns to the Holy Land.

48 This remains the case today: 'Orden de Montesa. Reseñas históricas', https://www.ordenesmilitares.es/orden-de-montesa/resenas-historicas /1394-2/ [accessed March 1, 2021].

Bibliography

Primary

Calderón, Fernando. *Hernán o la Vuelta del Cruzado.* Biblioteca Enciclopédica Popular, 70. Mexico City: Secretaría de Eduación Pública, 1945.

Gómez de la Cortina, José Justo. *Cartilla moral o método para estudiar la Historia.* Madrid: Eusebio Aguado, 1829.

———. Mexico City: Ignacio Cumplido, 1840.

———. Poliantea, Biblioteca del Estudiante Universitario, 46. Mexico City, UNAM, 1944.

Mariano Galván Rivera. *La Tierra Santa, o descripción exacta de Jope, Nazaret, Belén, el Monte de los Olivos, Jerusalén y otros lugares conocidos en el Evangelio, a lo quese agrega una noticia sobre otros sitios notables en la historia del pueblo hebreo.* 3 vols. Mexico City: Imprenta de M. Galván, 1842.

Pérez, Santiago. *Calendario nuevo de los Cruzados de la Nacional y Distinguida Orden Guadalupana, promovida y establecida por el libertador de la patria Don Agustín de Iturbide el año de 1822 y restaurada por su alteza serenísima, benemérito de la patria, general presidente Antonio López de Santa-Anna el año de 1853.* Mexico City: Imprenta de Santiago Pérez, 1855.

Secondary

Allen, David. 'Upholding Tradition: Benedict XIV and the Hospitaller Order of St. John of Jerusalem at Malta, 1740–1758'. *The Catholic Historical Review*, 0:1 (1984), pp. 18–35.

Blázquez Domínguez, Carmen. 'Veracruz: restablecimiento del federalismo e intervención norteamericana'. In Josefina Zoraida Vázquez (ed.), *México al tiempo de su guerra con Estados Unidos.* Mexico City: FCE/COLMEX/ SRE, 1998, pp. 559–77.

Borja Martínez, Ignacio. *Ilustre y distinguida Orden de Nuestra Señora de Guadalupe.* Mexico City: CONACULTA, 2011.

Cadenas y Vicent, Vincente (ed.). *Caballeros de Montesa que efectuaron sus pruebas de ingreso durante el siglo XIX.* 2nd ed. Madrid: Ediciones Hidalguía, 1995.

Ceballos-Escalera y Gila, Alfonso de. Antonio Sánchez de León y Cotoner and Dolores Palmero Pérez. *La Orden de Malta en España (1802–2002).* Palafox y Pezuela, 2002.

———. *La Real y Distinguida Orden Española de Carlos III.* Madrid: Presidencia del Gobierno/Real Casa de la Moneda/Boletín Oficial del Estado, 2016.

Cruz Barney, Óscar. 'Las Órdenes Militares en los Elementos Constitucionales de Ignacio López Rayón. Derecho premial en el movimiento insurgente de 1810'. https://archivos.juridicas.unam.mx/www/bjv/libros/7/3374/4. pdf [accessed February 26, 2021].

Fernández Fernández, Íñigo. 'El Liberalismo Católico en la prensa mexicana de la primera mitad del siglo XIX'. *Historia*, 1:396 (2014), pp. 59–74.

Gritzner, Maximilian. *Handbuch der Ritter- und Verdienstorden aller Kulturstaaten der Welt innerhalb des XIX. Jahrhunderts.* Leipzig 1893, Verlagsbuchhandlung J. J. Weber, reprinted Graz, 1962.

Hering Torres, Max Sebastián. *Rassismus in der Vormoderne. Die >Reinheit des Blutes< im Spanien der Frühen Neuzeit.* Frankfurt a. M. and New York: Campus, 2005.

Josserand, Philippe. 'The Templar Order in Public and Cultural Debate in France during the Eighteenth and Nineteenth Centuries'. In Helen Nicholson and Jochen Burgtorf (eds.), *The Templars, the Hospitallers and the Crusades. Essays in homage to Alan J. Forey.* London: Routledge, 2020, pp. 137–51.

Krebs Wilckens, Ricardo. *La Iglesia de América Latina en el siglo XIX.* Santiago de Chile: UCCh, 2002.

León Matamoros, María Graciela. 'El desamparo como argumento: mujeres en defensa de padres, esposos e hijos ante la ley de expulsión de españoles de 1829 en México'. *Amérique Latine Histoire et Mémoire. Les Cahiers AL-HIM*, 17 (2009), pp. 193–209.

Liehr, Reinhard. *Sozialgeschichte Spanischer Adelskorporationen. Die Maestranzas de Caballería (1670–1808) (Vierteljahrschrift für Sozial- und Wirtschaftsgeschichte. Beihefte, 70).* Wiesbaden: Franz Steiner Verlag, 1981.

Lohmann Villena, Guillermo. *Los Americanos en las Órdenes Nobiliarias*, 2nd ed., vol. 1. Madrid: CSIC, 1993.

Martínez Cosio, Leopoldo. *Los Caballeros de las Órdenes Militares en México.* Mexico City: Editorial Santiago, 1946.

Mayer, Hans Eberhard. 'America and the Crusades'. *Proceedings of the American Philosophical Society*, 125 (1981), pp. 39–45.

Michaud, Joseph François. *Histoire des Croisades*, 6th ed., vol. 6. Paris: Furne & Cie. Éditeurs, 1841.

Nieto Sánchez, Carlos. 'De la Ínclita Orden de San Juan de Jerusalén a la Asamblea Española: evolución de la Orden de Malta desde el siglo XIX hasta la actualidad'. In Javier Alvarado Planas and Jaime de Salazar Acha (eds.), *La Orden de Malta en España (1113–2013)*, vol. 1. Madrid: UNED/Salazar y Torres, 2015, pp. 481–518.

Nieto Sánchez, Carlos and Jaime de Salazar Acha. 'Caballeros de gracia españoles en la Orden de Malta (1802–1808)'. *Hidalguía*, CCCLVIII (2013), pp. 39–428.

Ortega y Medina, Juan Antonio (ed.). 'Discurso y cartas sobre varias reformas que parece deben hacerse en el método de algunos de nuestros estudios científicos. Polémica epistolar entre José Gómez de la Cortina y José María Lacunza'. In *Ortega y Medina: Polémicas y ensayos mexicanos entorno a la historia*, 3rd ed. Mexico: UNAM/IIH, 2001, pp. 79–150.

Pardo y Manuel de Villena, Alfonso and Suárez de Tangil y de Angulo, Fernando. *Índice de pruebas de los caballeros que han vestido el hábito de San Juan de Jerusalén (Orden de Malta) en el Gran Priorato de Castilla y León desde 1514 hasta la fecha.* Madrid: Librería de F. Beltrán, 1911.

Quirós Rosado, Roberto. 'Estratégicos anacronismos. Malta, la Orden de San Juan y la Corona española a fines del Antiguo Régimen (1795–1802)'. *Cuadernos de Historia Moderna,* 34 (2009), pp. 125–55.

Romero de Terreros y Vinent, Manuel. 'Las Órdenes Militares en México'. *Anales del Museo Nacional de Arqueología, Historia y Etnografía,* Tercera época, 16, IV (1912), pp. 199–235.

Rosas Salas, Sergio Francisco. 'Defender la independencia y soberanía de la Iglesia: El perfil del primer episcopado mexicano a través de Francisco Pablo Vázquez y Juan Cayetano Gómez de Portugal'. In Jesús Carlos Casas García and Pablo Mijangos y González (eds.), *Por una Iglesia libre en un mundo liberal. La obra y tiempos de Clemente de Jesús Munguía, primer arzobispo de Michoacán (1810–1888).* Mexico City: UPM/COLMICH, 2014, pp. 57–78.

Rossi, Antonio. *La Beata Vergine di Guadalupe e S. Stefano d'Aveto. Note e documenti.* Chiavari: Tipografia Artistica Colombo, 1910.

Roy, Joseph-Edmond. *L'Ordre de Malte en Amérique.* Quebec: Imprimerie Générale A. Coté et Cie, 1888.

Ruiz de Gordejuela Urquijo, Jesús. *La expulsión de los españoles de México y su destino incierto, 1821–1836.* Sevilla: Universidad de Sevilla, Escuela de Estudios Hispano-Americanos, Diputación de Sevilla, 2006.

Setton, Kenneth. *The Papacy and the Levant, vol. IV: The Sixteenth Century from Julius III to Pius V.* Philadelphia: The American Philosophical Society, 1984.

Stagno, Laura. 'Immacolata india. L'immagine della Vergine di Guadalupe messicana a Genova e in Liguria'. In Alessandra Anselmi (ed.), *L'immacolata nei rapporti tra l'Italia e la Spagna.* Rome: De Luca Editori d'arte, 2008, pp. 379–96.

Toomaspoeg, Kristjan. 'Die Geschichtsschreibung zu den mittelalterlichen geistlichen Ritterorden: status quaestionis'. In Karl Borchardt and Jan Libor (eds.), *Die geistlichen Ritterorden in Mitteleuropa.* Brno: Země a kultura ve střední Evropě, 2011, pp. 25–47.

Tyerman, Christopher. *The Debate on the Crusades, 1099–2010.* Manchester: Manchester University Press, 2011.

Vignau, Vicente and Uhagón, Francisco (eds.). *Índice de pruebas de los caballeros que han vestido el hábito de Santiago desde el año 1501 hasta la fecha.* Madrid: Tip. de la Viuda de M. Tello, 1901.

Zárate Toscano, Verónica. 'Tradición y modernidad: la Orden Imperial de Guadalupe, su organización y rituales'. *Historia Mexicana,* XLV, 2: 178 (1995), pp. 191–220.

6   The Internet Crusade against Communism

Political Neomedievalism in Twenty-first Century Brazil

Luiz Felipe Anchieta Guerra

Medieval Brazil?

There is no such thing as 'medieval Brazil'. Despite a certain histo-riographical lust for presenting feudal models for the Brazilian colonial economy or, more recently, seeking the medieval 'inheritances' of our culture, most researchers' consensus is that Brazil did not have a medieval period per se.[1] 'Discovered' and colonized by the modern Portuguese from 1500 onwards, Brazilian history is often divided, by its own scholars, into Pre-Discovery (up to 1500), Colony (1500–1822), Empire (1822–89), and Republic (from 1889 to the present day).[2]

This is mainly reflected in our schools' curriculum: the Middle Ages are only briefly taught and usually limited to a necessary transitional step in European history. A step between Classic and Modern times always related to understanding the importance of Religion, the permanence of Roman Structures, or how medieval labour structures compare to ancient and early modern ones.[3]

As a testament to the period's lack of prominence in the mainstream Brazilian curriculum, in 2015, historian Luís Fernando Cerri wrote an opinion that served as a basis for reducing and even excluding medieval and ancient history from the national syllabus. The opinion was grounded on a statistical analysis of data gathered by the *Jovens e a História* [Youth and History] Mercosul project, which supposedly 'proved' a sufficient knowledge of these periods by students between ages 15 and 16. Even though the said decision was quickly revoked and Cerri's methodology amply criticized by other researchers such as Prof. Claudia Bovo, this whole situation caused a commotion within the academic community, with most medievalists and classics historians taking a strong stance against it.[4]

That being said, the Middle Ages are, by no means, unknown to the average Brazilian. They are as much a part of the pop culture *zeitgeist*

DOI: 10.4324/9781003200802-7

over here as in most of the Western world. Medievalism has been a present aspect in literature, architecture, and culture. Furthermore, the same can be said about the recent revival of medieval popularity over the last decade: *Game of Thrones*' overwhelming success even spawned a medieval-themed Brazilian telenovela in 2018.

This recent surge also resulted in a particularly interesting boom of Brazilian political medievalism and neomedievalism from, at least, 2016 – most likely influenced in no small part by the uses of medieval imagery by Donald J. Trump's supporters in that year. Political medievalism in Brazil is not something new, with famous examples dating from the first decades of the twentieth century (such as Euclides da Cunha's *Os Sertões*). It is usually derived from the very traditional stereotype of the Dark Ages, with the medieval portrayed as something to overcome; more nostalgic appropriations, albeit rarer, are also not new (such as the uses of medieval imagery, since the 1960s, by the conservative Catholic group the Tradition, Family, Property movement, or TFP). However, what we are going to call political neomedievalism here is what is perhaps truly *nouveau*.

Political Neomedievalism?

Here we opt to distinguish between the more traditional forms of political medievalism and the phenomenon we will be calling political neomedievalism. If we follow available definitions of neomedievalism, it has been identified how this type of medievalism is not preoccupied with historical accuracy or what scholars have established as the 'real' Middle Ages. Instead, it creates a pseudo-medieval past that is neither new nor original – but appropriates known historical symbols and events to give them new contemporary meanings: just like the standard of Saint Maurice (a black saint) was used by white supremacist supporters in Charlottesville, USA, in 2017.[5]

On 'Past, Present and Neo', Richard Utz offers a very brief explanation of neomedievalism, providing us with a useful summary of Carol L. Robinson and Pamela Clements' original, and much more extensive, definition of the term, which points to the trauma which emerged when postmodernism further separated medievalism from its desired object.[6] We are aware that the aforementioned definitions were created to discuss works of fiction, like movies and games, and would not be the best fit to talk about political discourse and memes without some caveats. However, a single rigid definition of neomedievalism is very hard to establish, but as author KellyAnn Fitzpatrick points out, this might be one of its merits: the perpetual invitation to being defined.[7] Thus, we choose to adopt Utz's summary as the basis for the term here, but only as a starting point, and we will be referring to medievalisms like Crusader Donald Trump or the Charlottesville riot as political neomedievalisms, since they could be described, in Utz's terms, as 'neither an original nor the faithful copy of an original, but entirely "Neo"'.[8]

In this way, our perceptions of a 'medieval' past can be analogically compared with Lacan's mirror stage,[9] with the so-called 'real' Middle Ages being the original vase, hidden by physical obstruction (in this case, time itself), and therefore inaccessible and unattainable to all, even to historians themselves. After all, with all our methods and criteria, we scholars are, ultimately a product of our own time as well, ultimately plagued by our contemporary minds and thus incapable of the complete alterity needed to understand the past. In this scenario, the only form of seeing the hidden vase would be through its projection, the real, inverted image generated by the mirror, which already has some interference: this image we can call medievalism, since it can still be traced directly to the original vase, with all attempts to reach the Middle Ages being in some degree a form of medievalism itself. As French historian Nicole Loraux points out, it is impossible to access the past without interference from the present, and therefore the work of a historian is inherently anachronical.[10]

Neomedievalism, however, would be one step further, being the virtual image of said real image, which exists only inside the mirror, and which has already incorporated enough elements (such as the flowers in Lacan's drawings) and distortions to make sense on its own. It is a new image, an image of the image, a reflection of the reflection, a medievalism of medievalisms, which no longer needs to be linked to the original (historical period) to exist.

Utz's definition of neomedievalism also notes that it 'playfully obliterates history, authenticity, and historical accuracy', replacing its historical references with imagery already detached from the 'sources'. Moreover, this playfulness is a central aspect of political neomedievalism itself. Unlike political medievalism, which often presents itself in a more serious façade, aiming to connect with some supposed historical past, political neomedievalism centres itself around its own absurdity, evoking the language of memes to connect with its audience, and, therefore, requiring somewhat of an entertainment value, which is more important than the historical aspects themselves.

On a sidenote, about this attempted historicity, it is imperative to note that we are discussing intentions here. Therefore, we are not stating that the more traditional uses of the Middle Ages in political medievalism are necessarily more grounded on reality or even more accurate than their neomedievalism counterparts. Rather, we are pointing out that the preoccupation/necessity of being 'historical' is a fundamental characteristic of them. After all, one cannot deny that conspiratorial shows like History Channel's *Ancient Aliens* take their historical pretensions very seriously in their attempts to insert their narratives within historical contexts, no matter how twisted said attempts may be.[11] They might be doing 'bad history' as Andrew Elliott would call it,[12] but still they intend it to be historical, unlike the meme below:

In other words: within these political neomedievalistic materials, what matters most is the meme itself. Take, for example, Figure 6.1. In it, the Middle Ages themselves are not very important. What is

Figure 6.1 Brazil's President Jair Bolsonaro as a Knight Templar. The red star is the logo of the left-wing Workers' Party, the main rivals to Bolsonaro [author unknown].

essential is Bolsonaro's face, the sunglasses from the *deal with it* meme, and the four symbols around him – these are what conveys the message. He is, of course, dressed as a Templar Knight; in fact, this is even written in red on the image. However, that does not imply a pretence direct connection between him and the Templar Order or a Templar medieval past. The author of the meme is not really suggesting Bolsonaro to be related to the knights of old; in fact, we might say that the Templars here are used more an avatar of conservatism and order, than in reference to the historical military order.

Another aspect of this medieval meme culture is what we could call the retro-feeding effect. Due to the memes' swift nature, they tend to be direct responses or references to current events and also to one another. This often creates a correlation between progressive and conservative memes, both feeding into each other's medievalism. If

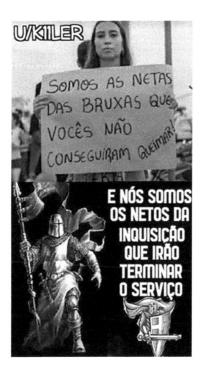

Figure 6.2 A Templar meme posted on Reddit by u/K11LER. The woman holds a sign reading 'We are the granddaughters of the witches that you could not burn'. Below, the text says 'And we are the grandsons of the Inquisition that will finish the job' [author unknown].

one side were to call Bolsonaro medieval, because he is antiquated, conservative, and a bigot (all medieval characteristics according to the Dark Ages stereotype), the other would then adopt this adjective, turning it into something positive: he is now medieval because he is strong, chivalrous, and masculine, for example.

Therefore, we are left with somewhat of a chicken-egg situation, in which it is almost impossible to determine who started it, but it is clear that they are both fundamentally interconnected. Perhaps, the most explicit example of this relationship is seen in the image below, Figure 6.2, in which we have the left-wing meme of being 'the granddaughters of the witches they could not burn' and its direct response from a Reddit user, in the form of a templar knight saying that they would finish the job now.

Lone Wolves or Organizations? From *Lux Brazil* to September 7, 2021

Even if this type of political meme is usually associated with scattered, independent, and mostly anonymous online content creators, to say that they are limited to that is a great understatement. In fact, this may only be the tip of the iceberg, since over the last few years more and more organized groups started to appear, not only taking credit for some of these creations but also trying to capitalize on them in order to organize rallies, protests, and even attacks.

This is truly 'uncharted territory', and a potentially profitable one at that. Since notions like authorship and ownership are very loose at best, when dealing with internet meme-culture,[13] it is often hard to identify how much said claims are warranted. The idea that these are not all lone wolves,[14] and that there may be some order to this chaos is a very important one, especially to confront the myth of disorganized white terrorism. However, there is always the risk of giving too much credit to certain groups and end up buying their own projected narratives of organization and influence.[15] After all, of course there is logic to chaos, but just how much of it?

To clarify this a bit more, let us now delve deeper into one of such groups, so-called *Institute Lux Brasil*: 'Patriots! I come from afar on a sacred quest. March 15, come with me, against the communists and traitors of the homeland. We will rescue our country, our flag. ORDINEN ET PROGRESSUS, VENIT AD LUX!'

In a short YouTube video, with these words, on March 3, 2020, a man supposedly dressed as a Knight Templar rallied Brazilians for a protest against Congress and the Supreme Court and in support of

President Jair Bolsonaro.[16] This small piece of promotion drew the attention of the entire Brazilian media and some international outlets as well, as some sort of bad joke, an unintentional caricature of the most delirious sectors of our far-right. This was Brazil's introduction to *Lux*.

Instituto Lux Brasil, the authors of the infamous video mentioned above, is a non-profit organization who presents itself as heir and defender of a conservative European Christian tradition, and, in an almost contradictory way, as apologists for modern liberal values. On their website their own description is: 'God, Country and Family are our core beliefs and values, in addition to the encouragement and recognition of: Minimum State; Pro-life; Conservation and maintenance of customs and traditions; Free market; Individual freedom'.[17]

Counting among its founders a notorious neo-Nazi historian, the *Lux* institute promotes a fierce revisionism of Brazilian history, having as one of its main guidelines the defence of the military dictatorship, and the 1964 coup.[18] For this, they make frequent use of neomedievalisms, going far beyond the aforementioned video. On their website one can see posters and other material produced by Lux, in which the figure of the Knight Templar is again evoked as an avatar of conservatism and the far-right.[19]

It is also very interesting to note that alongside said posters there are a couple of template versions available on the website as well.[20] These consist of banners with the *Lux* colour scheme, a bloody and battered templar knight with the *Lux* logo on the lower right corner, and the explanation that they are 'to have control of standardization in any type of media (banner, videos, texts, demonstrations, etc.) containing the *Lux Brasil* logo'. Here we can see a clear attempt to establish a brand, uniformizing and capitalizing, *a posteriori*, on the boom of political neomedievalisms we saw over the last years.

Lux might have produced one of the most iconic examples of Brazilian political neomedievalism, in the form of the 2020 video; however, the plans for continued content generated by associated members, with the use of said templates, apparently failed. This is evident on the institute's own website, which has barely been updated since late 2020. Despite achieving viral success early on, the *Lux* brand never really took off, and it seems to have been mostly abandoned since then.[21] In contrast to that, political neomedievalism never went away, it did not fade with the *Lux* brand. Quite the opposite, since it has continuously provided us with a seemingly endless stream of content for analysis, whose most notorious recent example is the 'Templar of Pernambuco', seen during the September 7, 2021 protests (Figure 6.3).

Figure 6.3 A Bolsonaro supporter dressed as a Templar at a demonstration in Recife, 2021 [Photo © @itsmepoan].

September 7, Brazil's Independence Day, is a date often associated with military parades and official celebrations. However, inspired by the riot at the US Capitol on January 6, 2021, President Bolsonaro and his supporters started a long campaign for most of 2021 to turn the Independence Day's celebrations into a show of force, intended to coerce and intimidate the opposition and perhaps even pave the way for an attempted coup d'état.[22] Whilst the more radical aspirations for the event seem to have failed, significant protests and demonstrations did happen in many Brazilian cities, and within them a picturesque figure stood out in the city of Recife: apparently unphased by the heat, one man stood strong in full 'Templar regalia', complete with leather boots and a dollar-store 'helmet'.

This figure's similarities to *Lux's* Templar are unlikely to be coincidental; however, no direct connection can be established between the two, other than that of a reference. This can be further witnessed in other neomedievalisms on display around September 7, such as Facebook banners advertised by the group *Templários da Pátria* [Templars of the Homeland] which summoned the 'good citizens' to the streets on Independence Day, to 'fight a crusade against the communist threat'.[23] These all share similarities in both tone and model to the *Lux* templates mentioned before. So, even if *Lux* ultimately failed to bottle up and brand these political neomedievalisms, it successfully left its influence all over them.

The Templars are not, however, the only reference to be found on said banners. From Solaire of Astora, a character from the *Dark Souls* videogame franchise, to Horatio Nelson and Uncle Sam *I want you* posters, they are filled to the brim with contemporary references which are, once again, much more relevant to the derivative product of neomedievalism than any historical medieval context. Even the 'crusade against communism' is likely more influenced (albeit indirectly) by the fundamentalist and integralist (*integrismo*, a political principle of Catholic faith) ideas of Plínio Corrêa, founder of the TFP movement, who in the 1960s proposed a crusade against modernity,[24] than by any medieval ideologies.[25] Going back to our Lacanian comparison and Utz's definition, neomedievalism does not require much (if any) knowledge of the Middle Ages to make sense on its own, it is a reflection of the reflection where the medieval is but a 'simulacrum'.[26]

Going back to our original question of just how much logic you can have in chaos, perhaps this can serve as an anecdotal answer. For it seems to illustrate well how all these productions of political neomedievalism are somewhat interconnected, and not the work of isolated individuals, but also how they are ultimately not on-demand products within a structured chain of production. Keeping true to their memetic aspects, these neomedievalisms seem to reproduce themselves organically, copied by imitation, influence, reference, and other methods, in a way that can never be fully controlled or predicted.[27] Hence, to decide between fully organized radical groups and lone wolves,[28] it might be best to consider a bit of both and take a more stochastic approach. The concept of Stochastic Terrorism is centred around acts that are not directly ordered through a clear chain of command but are also not the result of isolated individual actions. Instead, they are the statistical consequences of sufficiently reproduced ideas and discourses (i.e., the dehumanization of certain groups and individuals) that are analysable statistically but cannot be precisely predicted or controlled.[29] After all, as Molly Amman and J. Reid Meloy point out, Henry II neither participated in, nor ordered, the assassination Thomas Beckett, yet he is widely accepted as being responsible for it when he supposedly said 'Will no one rid me of this meddlesome priest?'.[30]

But Why Templars in Brazil?

After all we have seen, one thing still needs to be clarified, especially for those readers from outside of Brazil. Most of these political neomedievalisms tend to centre around the figure of the knight/crusader, often being referred to as 'Templar knights', and attempting to emulate that order's iconography. This begs the question: why the Templars? Well, there is a lot that can be said about the popularity of the Templar Order in present-day Brazil.

In fact, there are many 'Templar Orders' in modern Brazil, from loosely organized internet communities such as the *Templários da Pátria* to fully structured traditional orders tied to claims of nobility. A large portion of this can be attributed to one of the more traditional forms of Brazilian political medievalism: the Templar founding myth. This idea stems from the foundation of the Order of Christ in Portugal in 1319. This new military order was somewhat of a successor to the Templars in the Iberian Peninsula, inheriting their Portuguese lands and some of their personnel. The new order had deep ties with the Portuguese crown and nobility and, therefore, with their seafaring enterprises from the fifteenth century onwards.[31] This inspired many conspiracy theories about how the Templar Order secretly survived in Portugal, within the Order of Christ, and using their secrets and treasures managed to jumpstart the Age of Discovery.[32]

According to those theories, Brazil was then founded by Templar Knights, and their sacred mission continued here: a new crusade against pagans and heathens. This implicates a true denial of the colonization process, instead choosing to believe that Brazil was part of the Kingdom of Portugal as a territory of the Order of Christ, or in the worlds of self-styled historian Tito Lívio Ferreira:

> That's why he [the king of Portugal] soon baptized it with the name of Province of Santa Cruz, to be administered by the Portuguese Monarchy, independent of the Lusitanian Kingdom. Those fixated by European colonialism do not understand this, much less those limited by the Marxist idiom of historical materialism [...] an empty sophistry like a floating soap bubble. And they are happy to teach that Brazil was a colony, because Marx

is the atheist philosopher of the red economy, that is, of the class struggle, with the weapons of hatred and violence, with iron and fire, without documents.[33]

This idea is particularly strong around the city of São Paulo, whose flag still bears the red cross of the Order of Christ (Figure 6.4 below). And it grew in popularity around the early twentieth century as São Paulo consolidated its influence as the economic centre of Brazil.

Because of this, there are many 'official' Templar Orders in Brazil today who base their traditions in said inheritance, claiming to be the true descendants of the original order. Within these there are at least four structured 'Templar Orders' currently active in Brazil (and potentially many more smaller ones), with some of them even having some international recognition. These are the *Ordo Templum Domini*; the *Ordo Supremus Militaris Templi Hierosolymitani* O.S.M.T.H. BRASIL: *Grão Priorado de São Jorge*; O.S.M.T.H. *Gran Priorado Brasil: Cavalaria Espiritual São João Batista* (CESJB); *Gran Priorato Templário do Brasil: Cavalaria Espiritual São Francisco de Assis* (GPTB).[34] These groups often adopt masonic-like structures and symbols and award their members with titles such as Knight, Dame, Master, and

Figure 6.4 The flag of São Paulo city [Wikimedia Commons].

Grandmaster. All of them claim to be the one true representation of the Knights Templar in Brazil, and to be autonomous and independent Orders. They usually do not acknowledge each other.

The myth of a 'Templar connection' weighs heavily on the political uses of the Templar imagery here in Brazil, especially in those which we would classify as traditional political medievalisms. These, like the founding myth of São Paulo, or the New Crusade of the TFP, are deeply rooted in the idea that Brazil is, somehow, the inheritor of Western Christian Civilization.[35] However, even at their height these are somewhat fringe theories, which might be ingrained in the minds of certain groups but are far from being something most Brazilians would know or even recognize with at first. Therefore, whilst acknowledging its influence within Brazilian political medievalism, one cannot give these Templar conspiracy theories all the credit for the order's recurrent presence in Brazilian neomedievalisms.

In fact, the Templars are not only popular in Brazil. When dealing with neomedievalisms it is always important to remember that it is essentially a derivative product. Much like meme-culture, neomedievalisms do rely on a wide net of popular references that are required for it to make sense. Also, it is a product of capitalism and therefore bound by its laws of market, demand, and imperialism. Therefore, before looking at the Templars' popularity in Brazil, one must step back and see the Templars' popularity in the centres from where most cultural products are exported, especially the USA.

From the Trump electoral campaign in 2016 to the Capitol riot of 2021, the Templars are a popular form of US political medievalism as well. And part of that success can be attributed to the Templars' status on pop culture, as a successful brand of medievalisms; from books, to movies, to games, be they heroes or villains, the Templars are definitely among the most recognizable (even if completely inaccurate) medieval figures: the *über* knights.

This fascination with the Templar Order, as well as some of the shapes it took over the centuries is discussed in depth in Peter Partner's *The Murdered Magicians*,[36] but for here, suffice to say, that since the Templars are a very popular theme of medievalisms, it is to be expected that said popularity would reflect on how well they can work as an easily recognizable sign for the 'simulacra' of neomedievalism. Also, as the quintessential Christian knights, they are often associated with devotion, strictness, and, of course, the Crusades, elements which contribute to the order's attraction within far-right conservative groups.[37]

However, it still begs the question: why the Templars? All we have seen so far, in terms of popularity, could be attributed to the Templars' role as crusaders, but they are far from being the only group associated with the crusades, so why them specifically?

Well, in the case of Brazil, this can be in large part credited to the mythos that we have called the 'Templar connection', which might make the Templar Order more prominent. After all, their red crosses and the Order of Christ are a frequent presence on school textbooks and most depictions of colonial Brazil, not to mention within the city and the state of São Paulo. As for the wider prevalence of the Templars in pop culture, we can refer again to Peter Partner's much more in depth, albeit now a little dated, exploration of the subject.

However, there is another key component here, one that ought to be mentioned: the fact that the 'real' Templars are all dead and gone, and they have been that way for more than 700 years. This not only contributes to the mysticism of it all, but also makes them the perfect blank-slate archetype to be moulded for one's ideals and interests. After all, even if grossly misrepresented, there is no rightful or legal owner of the Templar brand to take action against it, which is definitely not the case for all other military orders, such as the Knights Hospitaller, the major successor orders of which operate a joint committee to take legal action against imitation orders.

This point is illustrated by a recent event in Brazil: during a Congress hearing in August 2021 about COVID vaccine overpricing, it was found that one of the investigated companies used the seal of the Knights Hospitaler on their website and in their documentation as if endorsed by them. This resulted in the Order of Malta sending an official note to the Brazilian Congress affirming that they had no connection to said company and had not authorized their brand to be used by it.[38]

Political Neomedievalism: A Dangerous Game

So, going back to our central point, political medievalism is clearly not a new phenomenon in neither Brazil nor the wider world. However, these more recent manifestations of 'alt-right Templars', as in the case of the *Lux Institute*, and the anonymous protester on Independence Day 2021, are, in a way, a new phenomenon within Brazil. Or at least new in terms of its popularization and prominence outside very specific niches such as the TFP, and also on how its characteristics are much more fitted to the subcategory of neomedievalism than to that of traditional political medievalism.

Although both episodes – with their respective costumes being much more adequate to a street carnival than to any historical Middle

Ages – may certainly seem to us like childish games and inexpressive daydreams, they are nonetheless a strong symptom of a much deeper phenomenon. The figure of the crusader, especially the Templar, appears to be increasingly consolidated within the national political imaginary,[39] and along with it we have a new resurgence of the Middle Ages as a stage for political disputes between different parts of the political spectrum. All of this in a country that, as we have established above, has no historical Middle Ages to speak of.

This political neomedievalism also directly translates another global phenomenon: the recent rise of a new conservative right-wing (often called the alt-right or alternative right) to power and the growing prominence of the media and forms of virtual language in the world of traditional politics. This phenomenon has as its major landmark the election of Donald J. Trump to the presidency of the USA in 2016,[40] and which produced its own neomedieval imagery boom during the campaign and even after.

Finally, it would be utterly naive to simply compare a meme of Jair Bolsonaro depicted as a Knight Templar to similar representations of any Western European leaders, and just assume that they are somewhat equivalent. Whilst the latter is appealing to a local nationalism and past, and an almost ancestral sense of belonging, the former is clearly not. Therefore, a post-colonial perspective becomes pivotal in the studies of Brazilian political medievalisms, to identify the Middle Ages as a foreign construct.

Thus, from September 7, 2021, to the *Lux's* Templar, passing through the various Brazilian web pages full of medieval 'political memes' – including the 'progressive' ones like André Dahmer's Medieval Brazil[41] – we see a Middle Ages full of completely anti-historical elements and connections. Templars burning witches, knights in sunglasses battling communism, none of these have any real bearing on the historical period known as the medieval. As historians and scholars, we know this very well; however, many of these memes' creators and overall 'Internet neo-Templars' are likely aware of it as well. This disconnection from the 'real' historical past should not be simply attributed to ignorance; on the contrary, it is fundamentally linked to the nature of such neomedieval contents, through which both progressives and conservatives dispute the meaning of a so-called medieval past that both wish to mobilize as a contemporary political instrument, and for which historical accuracy becomes a secondary, or even non-existent, concern.

There is methodological value in the distinction between political medievalism and neomedievalism, especially in the Americas, as there is a need to rethink scholarly approaches to certain uses of the past that tend to be more light-hearted/loose by their very nature (such as memes), treating them more seriously and not dismissing them as simple ignorance. And to understand that, as neomedievalisms often do, they care very little about the authenticity of the 'medieval' in them, and perhaps so should we. Instead choosing to focus on their more contemporary memetic elements and the many layers that detach them from the so-called Middle Ages, such as that of colonialism in the case of Brazil. After all, understanding these nuances might provide us with a broader grasp of how this 'playful' content might stochastically lead to very grim consequences.[42]

There is no such thing as 'Medieval Brazil'. The American Continent had no medieval past, and incorporating this element from our colonizers' history is, in a way, a perpetuation of the colonial discourse. Essentially, we would then be a little bit of Portugal in the Americas. Thus, thinking about the Middle Ages in Brazil, within the perspective of *longue durée*, can lead to dangerous situations in which fragments of 'primitive' Europe still live in the Badlands of our country. A place where, in the seventeenth century, 'Knights Templar' could crusade against indigenous infidels and communists. A land trapped in a different/foreign temporality, living in a time already lived by other parts of the world.

Notes

1 Frederic Mauro, *Le XVIe. Siècle Européen. Aspects Économiques* (Paris: Presses Universitaires de France, 1970), p. 352; Ruggiero Romano, 'American Feudalism', *Hispanic American Historical Review*, 64:1 (1984), p. 132; Luis Weckmann, *La Herencia Medieval del Brasil* (Mexico City, 1993).

2 An example of this periodization can be found at Sérgio Buarque de Holanda, *História geral da civilização brasileira* (São Paulo, 1985).

3 See Base Nacional Curricular Comum. MEC, 2015, pp. 415–21, basenacionalcomum.mec.gov.br/images/relatorios-analiticos/BNCC-APRESENTACAO.pdf [accessed 20 January 2022]; Base Nacional Curricular Comum. MEC, 2018, basenacionalcomum.mec.gov.br/images/BNCC_EI_EF_110518_versaofinal_site.pdf [accessed 20 January 2022].

4 Conducted since 2012, the Youth and History project in Mercosur is a multi-institutional initiative by Latin American researchers dedicated to making a quantitative survey on historical awareness, political culture, and learning perceptions of young people in the Mercosur countries; *Parecer para o texto preliminar do componente curricular História para a Base Nacional Comum Curricular* by Luíz Fernando Cerri was one of the nine opinions that based the 2015 BNCC's decision. Unfortunately, on the BNCC website, the opinion files are no longer available. Some of the replies to the aforementioned decision include a letter from the Brazilian Association of Medieval Studies (ABREM), web.archive.org/web/20160116063806/http://www.abrem.org.br/images/Carta_da_ABREM_sobre_a_BNCC.pdf.

5 Daniel Wollenberg, 'Defending the West: Cultural Racism and Pan-Europeanism on the Far-Right', *Postmedieval: A Journal of Medieval Cultural Studies*, 5:3 (2014), pp. 308–19.

6 Carol Robinson and Pamela Clements, 'Living with Neomedievalism', *Studies in Medievalism XVIII: Defining Medievalism(s) II*, ed. Karl Fugelso (Woodbridge, 2009), pp. 55–75; Carol L. Robinson and Pamela Clements, *Neomedievalism in the Media: Essays on Film, Television, and Electronic Games* (Lampeter, 2012).

7 KellyAnn Fitzpatrick, '(Re)producing (Neo)medievalisms', in *Studies in Medievalism XIX: Defining Neomedievalism(s) II*, ed. Karl Fugelso (Woodbridge, 2010), pp. 11–20.

8 Richard Utz, 'Past, Present and Neo', *Humanistic Perspectives in a Technological World*, ed. Richard Utz (Atlanta, 2014).

9 Jacques Lacan, 'The Mirror Stage as Formative of the Function of the I as Revealed in Psychoanalytic Experience', in *Écrits: A Selection*, trans. Alan Sheridan (Abingdon, 2001), pp. 146–78.

10 Nicole Loraux, 'Éloge de l'anachronisme en histoire', *Espace Temps*, 87–88 (2005), pp. 127–39.

11 Olav Hammer and Karen Swartz, 'Ancient Aliens', in *Handbook of UFO Religions*, ed. Ben Zeller (Leiden, 2021), pp. 151–77.

12 Andrew B. R. Elliott, 'Bad History and Contemporary Medievalism', *YouTube*, 2021, https://www.youtube.com/watch?v=0fWx4V1i0ps [accessed 20 January 2022].

13 Michael Soha and Zachary J. McDowell, 'Monetizing a Meme: YouTube, Content ID, and the Harlem Shake', *Social Media+ Society*, 2:1 (2016), pp. 1–12; Jakub Nowak, 'Internet Meme as Meaningful Discourse: Towards a Theory of Multiparticipant Popular Online Content', *Central European Journal of Communication*, 9:16 (2016), pp. 73–89.

14 Amy Kaufman and Paul Sturtevant, 'The Devil's Historians [Interview and round table] Linhas-UFRRJ', *Youtube*, 2020, https://www.youtube.com/watch?v=RSPnK1fqm6c&t=23s [accessed 20 January 2022].

15 Daniel Wollenberg, 'The New Knighthood: Terrorism and the Medieval', *Postmedieval: A Journal of Medieval Cultural Studies*, 5:1 (2014), pp. 21–33.

16 Lux Brasil, 'O cavaleiro da Lux convida você!...', *Youtube*, 4 March 2020, https://www.youtube.com/watch?v=JTQMu4TzoG4 [accessed 22 January 2022].

17 'Lux Brasil', https://luxbrasil.org.br/> [accessed 21 January 2022].

18 Cleber Lourenço, 'Uma brincadeira macabra: Instituto que gravou o "templário" brasileiro tem nazista em suas fileiras', *Forum*, 6 March 2020, https://revistaforum.com.br/blogs/ocolunista/uma-brincadeira-macabra-instituto-que-gravou-o-templario-brasileiro-tem-nazista-em-suas-fileiras/ [accessed 22 January 2022].

19 'Quem somos', https://luxbrasil.org.br/quem-somos/ [accessed 22 January 2022].

20 '1.png', https://luxbrasil.org.br/wp-content/uploads/2020/08/1.png [accessed 22 January 2022].

21 Thaís Monique Costa Moura, 'Um cavaleiro medieval em solo brasileiro: usos da idade média pela organização política Lux Brasil'. *1st International Conference Global Medievalisms*, 2021, https://www.youtube.com/watch?v=jA--79RdO_w&list=PLY_CJSkFcUSrSE2ZFVO-xBvR-9z7Qk2DW&index=12 [accessed 20 January 2022].

22 Andrew Fishman, 'Jair Bolsonaro's Pro-Coup Rally: September 7 Is Shaping Up to Be Brazil's January 6', *The Intercept*, 5 September 2021, https://theintercept.com/2021/09/05/bolsonaro-september-7-brazil-trump-january-6/ [accessed 20 January 2022].
23 Cf. the many neomedieval and Templar images on the group's Facebook page: 'Templários da Patria', *Facebook*, https://www.facebook.com/TemplariosDaPatria [accessed 25 January 2022].
24 Plinio Corrêa de Oliveira, *Revolução e contra-revolução* (1959); Roberto de Mattei, *O Cruzado do século XX Plinio Corrêa de Oliveira* (Porto, 1997).
25 Carlile Lanzieri Junior, *Cavaleiros de cola, papel e plástico: sobre os usos do passado medieval na contemporaneidade* (Campinas, 2021).
26 Alain Badiou, *Ethics – An Essay on the Understanding of Evil*, trans. Peter Hallward (London, 2001), p. 74.
27 J. T. Burman, (2012), 'The Misunderstanding of Memes: Biography of an Unscientific Object, 1976–1999', *Perspectives on Science*, 20:1 (2012), pp. 75–104; Susan Blackmore, 'Consciousness in Meme Machines', *Journal of Consciousness Studies*, 10:4–5 (2003), pp. 19–30; Richard Dawkins, *The Selfish Gene* (Oxford, 1976).
28 Ramón Spaaij, 'The Enigma of Lone Wolf Terrorism: An Assessment', *Studies in Conflict and Terrorism* 33:9 (2010), p. 866; Jacob Ware, *Testament to Murder: The Violent Far-Right's Increasing Use of Terrorist Manifestos* (International Centre for Counter-Terrorism, 2020).
29 Jakub Drmola and Tomáš Hubík, 'Stochastic Modeling of Non-linear Terrorism Dynamics', *Journal of Homeland Security and Emergency Management*, 18:3 (2021), pp. 251–81. Scott, Keith. 'Ha Ha Only Serious: Irony in Information Warfare and the Comedy-Cloaked Extremism'. *ICCWS 2021 16th International Conference on Cyber Warfare and Security* (2021).
30 Molly Amman and J. Reid Meloy, 'Stochastic Terrorism', *Perspectives on Terrorism*, 15:5 (2021), pp. 2–13. Contemporary chronicles disagree on what exactly Henry said, but that 'he uttered some such words is, however, beyond doubt': W. L. Warren, *Henry II* (London, 1973), p. 508.
31 For some historiographical views of the order's role in the Age of Discovery, see Bruno Tadeu Salles, 'A administração do Infante D. Henrique na Ordem de Cristo e os inícios da expansão marítima portuguesa no século XV (1420–1460)', *Revista Tempo de Conquista*, 4 (2008), pp. 1–25; ibid, 'A monarquia portuguesa nas discussões sobre o fim dos Templários e a fundação da Ordem de Cristo: aspectos das relações de poder entre D. Dinis, as Ordens Militares e o Papado (1314–1326)', *Revista Tempo de Conquista*, 1 (2007), pp. 1–15.
32 As seen in Tito Lívio Ferreira, *A Ordem De Cristo E O Brasil* (1980); Thales Veiga, *Histórias da Pátria Paulista* (2019).
33 Tito Lívio Ferreira, *A Ordem De Cristo E O Brasil* (1980), p. 53.
34 See Ordem Templaria Do Brasil, 'Ser Templário', https://templariosbrasil.org.br/avada_portfolio/ser-templario/ [accessed 20 January 2022]; O.S.M.T.H. Grão Priorado Brasil, 'O.S.M.T.H. Brasil', https://www.osmthbrasil.com/; Ordem dos Cavaleiros Templários Gran Priorato Templário do Brasil, 'Ordem dos Cavaleiros Templários – Home', https://www.granprioratotemplario.com.br/ [accessed 20 January 2022]; Ordem do Templo, Gran Priorato Templário do Brasil São Francisco de Assis – GPTB, 'Cavaleiros Templários do Brasil – Ordem do Templo Brasil', https://www.ordemdotemplobrasil.com/?lightbox=cf4t [accessed 20 January 2022].

35 Plínio de Oliveira, *Aspectos fundamentais da nobreza numa civilização cristã Catolicismo*, N° 549, Setembro de 1996.
36 Peter Partner, *The Murdered Magicians: The Templars and Their Myth* (Oxford, 1982).
37 Andrew B. R. Elliott, *Medievalism, Politics and Mass Media: Appropriating the Middle Ages in the Twenty-First century* (Woodbridge, 2017), pp. 132–54.
38 See the transcription of the official hearing, between timestamps 14:40 and 14:44, https://www25.senado.leg.br/web/atividade/notas-taquigraficas/-/notas/r/10111.
39 Raoul Girardet, *Mitos e mitologias políticas* (São Paulo, 1987).
40 Lise Esther Herman, *Trumping the Mainstream* (Abingdon, 2019).
41 André Dahmer, 'O Brasil Medieval. Um fio com algumas tiras da série.', *Twitter*, https://twitter.com/malvados/status/1422572618587283456 [accessed 19 January 2022].
42 Keith Scott, 'Ha Ha Only Serious: Irony in Information Warfare and the Comedy-Cloaked Extremism'. *ICCWS 2021 16th International Conference on Cyber Warfare and Security* (2021).

Bibliography

Amman, Molly, and J. Reid Meloy. 'Stochastic Terrorism'. *Perspectives on Terrorism*, 15:5 (2021), pp. 2–13.

Badiou, Alain. *Ethics – An Essay on the Understanding of Evil*. trans. Peter Hallward. London: Verso, 2001.

Blackmore, Susan. 'Consciousness in Meme Machines'. *Journal of Consciousness Studies*, 10:4–5 (2003), pp. 19–30.

Burman, J. T. 'The Misunderstanding of Memes: Biography of an Unscientific Object, 1976–1999'. *Perspectives on Science*, 20:1 (2012), pp. 75–104.

Dawkins, Richard. *The Selfish Gene*. Oxford: Oxford University Press, 1976.

Drmola, Jakub, and Tomáš Hubík. 'Stochastic Modeling of Non-linear Terrorism Dynamics'. *Journal of Homeland Security and Emergency Management*, 18:3 (2021), pp. 251–81.

Elliott, Andrew B. R. *Medievalism, Politics and Mass Media: Appropriating the Middle Ages in the Twenty-First Century*. Woodbridge: Boydell & Brewer, 2017.

———. 'Bad History and Contemporary Medievalism'. *YouTube* (2021), https://www.youtube.com/watch?v=0fWx4V1i0ps [accessed 20 January 2022].

Ferreira, Tito Lívio. *A Ordem De Cristo E O Brasil*. IBRASA, 1980.

Fitzpatrick, KellyAnn. '(Re)producing (Neo)medievalisms'. In *Studies in Medievalism XX: Defining Neomedievalism(s) II*. ed. Karl Fugelso. Woodbridge: Boydell & Brewer, 2010, pp. 11–20.

Girardet, Raoul. *Mitos e mitologias políticas*. São Paulo: Companhia das Letras, 1987.

Hammer, Olav, and Karen Swartz. 'Ancient Aliens'. In *Handbook of UFO Religions*. ed. Ben Zeller. Leiden: Brill, 2021, pp. 151–77.

Herman, Lise Esther. *Trumping the Mainstream*. Abingdon: Routledge, 2019.

Holanda, Sérgio Buarque de. *História geral da civilização brasileira*. São Paulo: Difel 2, 1985.

Kaufman, Amy, and Paul Sturtevant. 'The Devil's Historians'. *Linhas-UFRRJ* (2020), https://www.youtube.com/watch?v=RSPnK1fqm6c&t=23s [accessed 20 January 2022].

Lacan, Jacques. *Écrits: A Selection*. trans. Alan Sheridan. Abingdon: Routledge, 2001.

Lanzieri Junior, Carlile. *Cavaleiros de cola, papel e plástico: sobre os usos do passado medieval na contemporaneidade*. Campinas: D7 Editora, 2021.

Loraux, Nicole. 'Éloge de l'anachronisme en histoire'. *Espace Temps*, 87–88 (2005), pp. 127–39.

Lourenço, Cleber. 'Uma brincadeira macabra: Instituto que gravou o "templário" brasileiro tem nazista em suas fileiras'. *Forum*. 6 March 2020, https://revistaforum.com.br/blogs/ocolunista/uma-brincadeira-macabra-instituto-que-gravou-o-templario-brasileiro-tem-nazista-em-suas-fileiras/ [accessed 22 January 2022].

Mattei, Roberto de. *O Cruzado do século XX Plinio Corrêa de Oliveira*. Porto: Editora Civilização, 1997.

Mauro, Frederic. *Le XVIe. Siècle Européen. Aspects Économiques*. Paris: Presses Universitaires de France, 1970.

Moura, Thaís Monique Costa. 'Um cavaleiro medieval em solo brasileiro: usos da idade média pela organização política Lux Brasil'. *1st International Conference Global Medievalisms, 2021*, 2021, https://www.youtube.com/watch?v=jA--79RdO_w&list=PLY_CJSkFcUSrSE2ZFVO-xBvR-9z7Qk2DW&index=12 [accessed 20 January 2022].

Nowak, Jakub. 'Internet Meme as Meaningful Discourse: Towards a Theory of Multiparticipant Popular Online Content'. *Central European Journal of Communication*, 9:16 (2016), pp. 73–89.

Oliveira, Plinio Corrêa de. *Revolução e contra-revolução*. Rio de Janeiro: Boa Imprensa, 1959.

Oliveira, Plínio de. *Aspectos fundamentais da nobreza numa civilização cristã Catolicismo*. N° 549, Setembro de 1996.

Partner, Peter. *The Murdered Magicians: The Templars and their Myth*. Oxford: Oxford University Press, 1982.

Robinson, Carol, and Pamela Clements. 'Living with Neomedievalism'. In *Studies in Medievalism XVIII: Defining Medievalism(s) II*. ed. Karl Fugelso. Woodbridge: Boydell & Brewer, 2009, pp. 55–75.

———. *Neomedievalism in the Media: Essays on Film, Television, and Electronic Games*. Lampeter: Edwin Mellen Press, 2012.

Romano, Ruggiero. 'American Feudalism'. *Hispanic American Historical Review*, 64:1 (1984), pp. 121–34.

Salles, Bruno Tadeu. 'A administração do Infante D. Henrique na Ordem de Cristo e os inícios da expansão marítima portuguesa no século XV (1420–1460)'. *Revista Tempo de Conquista*, 4 (2008), pp. 1–25.

————. 'A monarquia portuguesa nas discussões sobre o fim dos Templários e a fundação da Ordem de Cristo: aspectos das relações de poder entre D. Dinis, as Ordens Militares e o Papado (1314–1326)'. *Revisto Tempo de Conquista*, 1 (2007), pp. 1–15.

Scott, Keith. 'Ha Ha Only Serious: Irony in Information Warfare and the Comedy-Cloaked Extremism'. *ICCWS 2021 16th International Conference on Cyber Warfare and Security.* Academic Conferences Limited, 2021.

Soha, Michael, and Zachary J. McDowell. 'Monetizing a meme: YouTube, content ID, and the Harlem Shake'. *Social Media+ Society*, 2:1 (2016), pp. 1–12.

Spaaij, Ramón. 'The Enigma of Lone Wolf Terrorism: An Assessment'. *Studies in Conflict and Terrorism*, 33:9 (2010), pp. 854–70.

Utz, Richard. 'Past, Present and Neo'. In *Humanistic Perspectives in a Technological World.* ed. Richard Utz. Atlanta: Georgia Institute of Technology, 2014.

Veiga, Thales. *Histórias da Pátria Paulista. Cultura Território e Governos.* Santos: Editora Comunicar, 2019.

Ware, Jacob. *Testament to Murder: The Violent Far-Right's Increasing Use of Terrorist Manifestos.* The Hague: International Centre for Counter-Terrorism, 2020.

Warren, W. L. *Henry II.* London: Eyre Methuen, 1973.

Weckmann, Luis. *La Herencia Medieval del Brasil.* Mexico City: Fondo de Cultura Económica, 1993.

Wollenberg, Daniel. 'Defending the West: Cultural racism and Pan-Europeanism on the far-right'. *Postmedieval: A Journal of Medieval Cultural Studies*, 5:3 (2014), pp. 308–19.

————. 'The New Knighthood: Terrorism and the Medieval'. *Postmedieval: A Journal of Medieval Cultural Studies*, 5:1 (2014), pp. 21–33.

Index

www.ingramcontent.com/pod-product-compliance
Ingram Content Group UK Ltd.
Pitfield, Milton Keynes, MK11 3LW, UK
UKHW020421010325
455677UK00029B/964